D0307753

# RITUALS TO CHANGE YOUR LIFE

## DAILY PRACTICES TO BRING GREATER INNER PEACE AND HAPPINESS

### THERESA CHEUNG

WATKINS

Sharing Wisdom Since
1893

This edition first published in the UK and USA 2017 by
Watkins, an imprint of Watkins Media Limited
19 Cecil Court
London WC2N 4EZ

enquiries@watkinspublishing.com

Design and typography copyright © Watkins Media Limited 2017

Text copyright © Theresa Cheung 2017

Theresa Cheung has asserted her right under the Copyright, Designs
and Patents Act 1988 to be identified as the author of this work.

1 3 5 7 9 10 8 6 4 2

Designed and typeset by JCS Publishing Services Ltd,
www.jcs-publishing.co.uk

Printed and bound in Finland

A CIP record for this book is available from the British Library

ISBN: 978-1-78028-987-8


www.watkinspublishing.com

# C O N T E N T S

Acknowledgements        vii
Introduction: 21 Days        viii

PART I: WAKE WITH DETERMINATION
7 LIFE-CHANGING MORNING RITUALS        1

Life-Changing Ritual #1: Wake Up Earlier        3
Life-Changing Ritual #2: Stretch Instead of Reaching
    for Your Phone        15
Life-Changing Ritual #3: Ask Yourself One Simple
Question        25
Life-Changing Ritual #4: Just Breathe        35
Life-Changing Ritual #5: Smile in the Mirror        42
Life-Changing Ritual #6: See the Finish Line        50
Life-Changing Ritual #7: Tune In        60
Morning Check Point        68

PART II: LIVE ON PURPOSE
7 LIFE-CHANGING DAYTIME RITUALS        69

Life-Changing Ritual #8: Tidy One Thing        71
Life-Changing Ritual #9: Fill Your Own Cup        82
Life-Changing Ritual #10: Let It Go        91
Life-Changing Ritual #11: Say a Little Prayer        101
Life-Changing Ritual #12: Light Someone Up        111
Life-Changing Ritual #13: Listen, Really Listen        123
Life-Changing Ritual #14: Right Here, Right Now        127
Daily Check Point        138

PART III: RETIRE WITH SATISFACTION
7 LIFE-CHANGING EVENING RITUALS                     139

Life-Changing Ritual #15: Over to You           141
Life-Changing Ritual #16: Say Grace             147
Life-Changing Ritual #17: Write It Down         153
Life-Changing Ritual #18: Higher Selfie         159
Life-Changing Ritual #19: Repeat After Me       164
Life-Changing Ritual #20: Flash Forward         171
Life-Changing Ritual #21: Say Thank You         176
Evening Check Point                             180

Afterword: The Adventure Begins...              181
References                                      184
Select Bibliography                             192
About the Author                                194

# ACKNOWLEDGEMENTS

Sincere gratitude to my editor, Jo Lal, for being the inspiration behind this book and to Etan Ilfeld for his kindness and support. Thanks also to Sandy Draper for her invaluable help and input at developmental copy-edit stage and to everyone at Watkins Media involved in the production of this book. I couldn't be happier and feel more privileged to be given the opportunity to work with a publisher that has such an awesome history and reputation in the world of mind body spirit.

Heartfelt thanks to book blogger Kim Nash (www. kimnash.co.uk), who helps run my social media with inspiration and joy every single day. And, as always, my deepest gratitude and love to Ray, Robert and Ruthie for their love, patience and understanding, as I immersed myself in the life-transforming ritual of writing this book.

# INTRODUCTION

# 21 DAYS

'You are what you repeatedly do.'

Aristotle

A few years ago I watched an intriguing mind-game experiment on TV, hosted by the ingenious magician and hypnotist Derren Brown. A group of people were put in a room and told that the door would only be unlocked when certain clues were deciphered. The experiment began and everybody in the room focused their intention on solving the clues – number sequences, flashing lights and so on – but to no avail. When the allotted time for the experiment ended an announcement was made: every 'door unlocking' clue given during the experiment had been totally meaningless and unsolvable, and the door had been unlocked within moments of the experiment starting. Nobody in the room had thought to check if the doors were actually locked. They just assumed they were. Anyone in that room could simply have opened the door and walked out at any time!

In brief, that is what this book is all about. There is an astonishingly simple way to change our lives for the better but most of us haven't paid attention to it because it is so glaringly obvious. We assume life is outside our control, or we can change it by changing our thoughts, but the simplest and most effective way to make our lives better is to change what we repeatedly do every day – starting today.

Most of us have absolutely no idea that what we repeatedly do creates our everyday experience. We think our future is shaped by big events, decisions we make, thoughts we have, and opinions of others, but this book will show you that it is your daily actions that are the golden key. Pay close attention to what you actually do every day and see your life transform.

Even those of us who are aware of the impact daily actions can have on our wellbeing and fulfilment, we often still don't fully understand their life-changing potential. We know that certain things, such as journaling or deep breathing, can make us feel better but we aren't quite sure why. One teacher tells us to practise gratitude, another tells us to meditate, others have different approaches and recommendations, but which is right? All the advice seems so vague and disconnected and only seems to work sporadically at best. Despite our good intentions, our lives remain essentially unchanged.

However, if an action is repeated often enough it becomes a habit, although this book isn't about establishing positive habits either, as habits can't connect you to a field of infinite possibility and therefore can't change your life. To attract love, success and happiness, research shows that your daily actions need to be filled with a sense of sacred meaning and power – they need to be ritualized.

If practised for a minimum of 21 days, every ritual in this book will absolutely change your life for the better. Incorporate all the rituals into your life, most of which can be performed in a matter of moments, and you will notice positive change. This book will prove to you that you are what you do. You will be left in no doubt that your daily rituals have astonishing life-changing power.

## DOING IS BEING

'Ritual is to the internal sciences what experiment is to the external sciences.'

Timothy Leary

You'd have had to have been living under a stone not to have come across the self-help concept of your thoughts having the power to create your world. Popularized by Rhonda Byrne and her million-selling title, *The Secret*, there is profound truth in this concept but also a serious problem. Has positive thinking ever truly worked for you?

Have you repeated your affirmations and decluttered all that negative thinking and sent cosmic orders out into the universe but your life hasn't improved or changed? Be honest now – has this lack of progress made you question whether positive thinking really works?

Most of us do understand the importance of positive thinking and the principle of like attracts like. We try to monitor that voice in our head and transform negative into positive but in reality it doesn't really matter how positive your thoughts are if that positivity doesn't impact your daily routines. To risk repeating myself, it is what you actually do with your life, not what you think about your life, that is transformative.

When I started my writing career I was relentlessly positive. In my mind I saw myself getting contract after contract and writing books that inspired people. In reality I spent my days writing about topics I wasn't fully engaged in and the result was that nobody fully engaged with my writing. In fact it took me a couple of decades to finally get the obvious: I needed to start doing what I was thinking about. I needed to write about what I loved and not what other people thought I should write about. The result – two *Sunday Times* top 10 bestsellers.

## THE MISSING LINK

'A daily ritual is a way of saying I'm voting for myself, I'm taking care of myself.'

Mariel Hemingway

Yes, thoughts create reality and there is an invisible power in the universe you can tap into with your thoughts to heal and prosper. Understanding this fundamental spiritual concept is, however, only one half of the 'attract success into your life' equation. The other half is just as important but neglected because it is so obvious. The missing link here is that your daily actions need to be as life affirming as your thoughts. What you do needs to reflect what you think. Your actions need to attract good things into your life in the same way your thoughts do.

Recent research from the University of California shows that your brain is led by your actions[1] so perhaps your daily routines should be the first place you start because if your daily actions are positive then your thoughts will follow. Remember, you are what you think isn't the full story, as you are also what you repeatedly do.

For the next 21 days you have the rare opportunity to completely transform your life and attract good things into your life – whether that is love, money, success, better health or peace of mind – by making simple changes in your daily routine.

Take me, for example: a while ago I felt taken for granted and unappreciated. I was always smiling, helping and going that extra mile but I didn't feel respected by others in return. Then I made the decision to spend a few minutes each day writing in a gratitude journal and really focus on that concept of being thankful. Within three weeks it felt like everyone's attitude toward me had changed. People smiled at me, my children started helping around the house (all unprompted) and my editor sent me a surprise bunch of flowers on the publication of one of my books.

It was the same story for my health. I don't get ill often but when I do I can't help but feel like I have failed in some way and that negative thinking has lowered my immunity. Last year I went down with a terrible flu that everybody, including my doctor, said would wipe me out for at least two weeks. I spent the first few days trying to carry on with my routine as normal and telling myself I could fight this and get better. I got worse. Then I stopped telling myself I would heal soon and took action instead. I made the decision to take a week completely off work to give my mind and body a chance to heal. I unplugged my phone, treated myself to some silence and peace, and was completely better within three days.

## THE POWER OF 'I DO'

'Be the change you want to see in the world.'

Mahatma Gandhi

The 21 rituals in this book, which should be practised for a minimum of 21 days (more about the importance of that magic number 21 a little later), will prove to you that actions speak louder than thoughts or words when it comes to attracting success and happiness into your life. They will prove what scientists and psychologists from all over the world over the past few decades have discovered – that there is far more power in 'I do' than 'I think'.[2] Every action we take impacts our thoughts and fills them with the power to create a life of infinite possibility.

However, to tap into that infinite possibility you have to make a commitment to the rituals. You can't be half-hearted and only do them when you feel like it or remember. After all, who wants to help someone who is half-hearted? You wouldn't support a runner, for example, who kept quitting halfway through the race. Yet that is how many of us commit to changing our daily routines. Why would the universe respond?

This book will not only explain the life-changing power of 'I do' but doing the rituals will also prove how actions rather than thoughts get the universe on your side. You'll learn that understanding the meaning of a ritual and putting it into action will attract all sorts of amazing things into your life. You may also find that you'll get rid of those nagging doubts that something you are thinking or something about you, but you aren't sure what, is wrong with you. You will just know that you are in charge of your life and what happens in it.

There wasn't an exact moment in my life when I suddenly realized that all the positive thinking and law of attraction exercises, books and mantras I had been fascinated with for most of my adult life were not working. I do know today that it is my 'just do it' philosophy that is bringing into my life all that I have dreamed of.

For years I started making small changes in my life and seeing positive results but the moment that convinced me actions speak louder than words is something that I think of as a personal breakthrough. In my books I often talk about the importance of self-love for success and happiness. I often recommend some exercises or mantras. Then one day my assistant, Kim, suggested I start posting short videos on my Facebook author page about my writing. Having been an invisible writer for so long, I was absolutely terrified of going public. I did a few practice videos on my mobile but none of them felt right. Kim kept asking me to send one over but I kept making excuses and saying I needed more time to think. I didn't need time. The truth was I was worried about how I would be perceived. Eventually she said I should just post something and then went on to say that clearly I didn't have enough self-love and self-belief. I wasn't living my message.

The words really stung but that was because she was right. I needed to just do it and love myself enough to not take it personally if the reaction was negative. So before I recorded my first short message I told myself that I loved who I was and it did not matter what others thought about how I came across. I smiled at myself in the camera, took a selfie and said with as much conviction as I could muster, 'I love you.' Then I recorded a short video and posted it. The reaction online was encouraging. In the weeks ahead I repeated the same self-love ritual before each video I released. Viewer numbers grew and grew (with one of my videos climbing to 130,000 views overnight and no negative comments), as my trust in myself grew. It was astonishing. I realized then that all those years of telling myself with my thoughts that I should love myself more had not convinced the universe. I needed to show – or spell out to the universe with my actions – that I was proud of who I was.

Since then I have truly understood the life-changing power of ritual.


## THE POWER OF RITUAL

'Ritual is the way you carry the presence of the sacred. Ritual is the spark that must not go out.'

Christina Baldwin


I must now stress the very real and significant difference between ritual and habit, as this is a book about the power of ritual, not habit. Habits are mindless activities done without conscious thought and intention, and therefore unlikely to impress the universe. Rituals, on the other hand, are activities filled with a sense of sacredness because when you perform them you assign deep personal meaning to them, and as such they are magnets for success and happiness.

To transform a habit into a ritual you have to fill it with a sense of sacred meaning. You have to make something ordinary feel extraordinary, something mundane feel sacred, and this book will show you how to do that.

There is plenty of research to prove that rituals have the power to change lives. A recent series of investigations by psychologists from Lancaster University has revealed intriguing new results demonstrating that personal rituals can and do have a causal impact on people's thoughts, feelings and behaviour.[3] Every one of the rituals in this book is backed by scientific research and I'll be referring to some of it throughout the book. (Please also refer to the Select Bibliography on page 192.)

## THE POWER OF 21

'Once you've installed a ritual or a new habit, you don't have to use any willpower.'

Robin Sharma

Psychologist Maxwell Maltz was a plastic surgeon in the 1950s and he began to notice that it took around 21 days for his patients to get used to seeing their new face This observation then prompted him to think about his own adjustment period to new behaviours and he noticed it took a minimum of 21 days to form a new habit. In 1960 he relayed this information in his million-copy-selling book, *Psycho-Cybernetics*, and from that moment onwards 21 became the magic number and inspiration for positive change.

Since then there has been other research, most recently a study led by health psychology researcher Phillippa Lally, published in the *European Journal of Social Psychology*, which has shown that 21 days is the absolute minimum requirement to form a new behaviour.[4] But regardless of whether or not a new behaviour has been firmly established, think of 21 days as a symbolic landmark, because by that time it is likely that you will have started to experience the positive benefits of your new routine and feel empowered enough to continue.

In addition, the number 21 is pretty significant in the esoteric arts too. In numerology 21 is made up of the vibration of the 2 and 1. Number 1 is all about new beginnings, independence, uniqueness, striving forward, progress, attainment, achievement and success. Number 2 is all about encouragement, cooperation and finding balance. Put the numbers together in a numerology chart and an abundance of energy, new opportunities, exciting directions and transformation is suggested. In Paganism too the 21-day full moon ritual is a potent way to create a new belief system.

Remember, this book isn't about changing habits but about incorporating rituals into your life and rituals are habits you fill with sacred meaning, so getting to 21 days has profound meaning because, thanks to Maltz and the esoteric arts, we associate that number with positive change.

## GETTING YOUR CONSCIOUS MIND ON BOARD

'Live your daily life in a way that you never lose yourself.'
Thich Nhat Hanh

To ensure a habit becomes entrenched at the neural level – and is therefore powerful enough to trigger positive change – you have to start at day one and be motivated to continue for three weeks. You don't need to tell yourself this is going to be forever, just 21 days. Then at the end of that time you have a choice about whether you continue or you don't. The chances are you will continue because new neural pathways will have formed in your brain and you will already be seeing benefits. However, you need to give your conscious mind that opportunity to choose because it always likes to think it is in charge. If you tell your conscious mind that this new ritual is for life then it is likely to rebel because it hasn't yet seen the long-term benefits. You need to prove to your conscious mind that the benefits are real first.

And if you think all this talking to yourself is verging on the strange – it really isn't. We talk to ourselves in our heads all the time and the positive-thinking movement built a self-help industry around this self-talk.

Your conscious or logical mind is unlikely to be convinced but this next piece of information might speak to your unconscious mind – the place where the world of possibility first reaches out to us.

## RECAP

Consciously creating symbolic acts ensures you have the tools to shift your mind-set, break through barriers, open yourself to an expanded version of yourself and attract unlimited success and happiness into your life. However, for a ritual to truly impact your life remember it is absolutely vital that you repeat it daily for a minimum of 21 days – the minimum time for an activity to imprint itself on your brain and become a natural part of your life.

## PUTTING IT ALL TOGETHER

'Any ritual is an opportunity for transformation.'

Starhawk

In the pages that follow you'll see science, psychology and spirit blend together to create a new path to transformation. For each of those days you will perform 21 simple rituals.

You'll do seven in the morning, seven in the afternoon and seven at night so that your entire day is focused toward attracting positive change and abundance into your life.

The format of this book will match the pattern of your day with a burst of energy and information to take on board for your wake-up rituals, followed by a steady supply of motivation and advice for your daily rituals and then a reduction in the amount of information to process with some simple, gentle rituals to help you wind down with satisfaction before retiring to bed.

## WAKE WITH DETERMINATION

Starting your day right is the foundation stone upon which everything rests. Basically, what you are doing is waking up each day on purpose and dedicated to fulfilling the infinite potential that is within you. The seven morning rituals recommended here will attract success and happiness your way and prove that when you change the way you wake up you change your entire life.

## LIVE ON PURPOSE

The seven rituals to be performed in the afternoon are all about keeping you focused and on track so that every thought you have and action you take continue to attract unlimited possibility your way.

## RETIRE WITH SATISFACTION

Ending your day on a note of satisfaction with the help of the seven rituals suggested here will help you recharge fully so that when you wake up the next day you will be bursting with energy to become the happiest, most successful and most amazing person you can possibly be.

## YOU ARE THE PROOF

'Happiness doesn't come from big pieces of great success,
but from small advantages hammered out day by day.'

Jim Rohn

When it comes to meeting goals in life recent research from the American Psychological Association shows that our daily routines are more important than self-discipline and self-control, and for the next 21 days I'm going to ask you to prove the power of ritual to change your life for the better. You will feel at your peak each and every day and stay there – having the best day of your life every day.

In 1983 Tony Robbins wanted to change his life with a passion. He had hit rock bottom. He felt like a complete failure. Physically, emotionally, mentally and spiritually he felt inadequate and drained. He was overweight, depressed and living alone in a small flat with no kitchen so he washed his dishes in the bathtub.

He decided he could not live like this anymore so he did something that changed his whole life. He changed his way of thinking and his routines, and the first one he established was writing a journal. He wrote down all the things in his life he didn't want any more and all the things he did want. In his own words, 'I set aside all my limiting beliefs and sat down on the beach with my journal.'

For the next few hours he wrote continuously about what his ideal life would be and gave himself a time limit to achieve those goals as anytime from tomorrow to the next 20 years. He did not pause to think about whether these goals were possible but simply wrote them down. In the coming days and weeks he started to create milestones that he could work towards and he returned to his journal time and time again to define what kind of person he wanted to become and the future of his dreams.

Even Tony was shocked by just how many of the milestones he had written in his journal started to come true in a short space of time. Simply writing down his goals helped him create clarity about his future and totally transformed his life. Not only did he write several million-selling self-help books, but he also became the world's most recognized, successful and influential life coach.

That is what I hope *21 Rituals to Change Your Life* will do for you. I hope it will change your life for the better in every possible way. I hope it will inspire you to prove that you are what you do, anything is possible for you and happiness and success is a choice you make every single day.

## THE PROVEN BENEFITS OF RITUAL

'Life feels empty without ritual.'

Anonymous

Research validates that just having more rituals in your life is actually the most important part.[5] It is not so much what the ritual is, but that it is *your* ritual and, according to Harvard professor Francesco Gino, author of *Sidetracked: Why Our Decisions Get Derailed and How We Can Stick to the Plan*, the more personal you make it and the more consistent you are with it, the more powerful it will be.

Often we just rush mindlessly through life but ritual truly can have a profound impact on how you feel and how well you perform. If you have ever performed a toast before having a drink, or sang 'Happy Birthday' before blowing out candles on a birthday cake, that's a ritual that focuses your attention on what you drink or eat and as a result you enjoy it more. It's called savouring the moment and studies show that savouring is one of the most important happiness boosters.[6-8] Present-moment awareness is also very much a part of the mindfulness movement that you may have heard about recently.

Other research shows how the ritual of expressive writing truly can help you feel better, especially during times of grief and loss.[9] Personal rituals have also been proven to reduce anxiety before an important event. Even crazy rituals – like wearing lucky socks – can have a powerful effect on outcome. Again it doesn't matter what the ritual is, what matters is how the ritual makes you feel.

If you are starting to feel sceptical about all this research demonstrating the power of personal ritual at this point it doesn't really matter. What is even more exciting about this research is that it has shown that belief in the power of the ritual isn't essential.[10-12] Obviously rituals work better alongside the power of belief but if you aren't convinced, they can still work. What matters is that it is a ritual you understand the meaning of personally and, even more important than that, it is a ritual that you actually do.

The most effective rituals are not ones associated with religion, celebrities or sporting icons but those associated with you and your heart, and *your* heart alone.


## WHY WE MISSED THE OBVIOUS

'It's a simple ritual, but it has so many benefits.'

Miriam Weinstein

Let me take you back to the beginning of the book when I mentioned the closed-door experiment and how everybody focused on the 'door unlocking' clues given but nobody tried the obvious which was to check if the door was actually locked (see page viii). This is what we have tended to do in the self-help movement in recent years – we have focused all our attention and energy on our thoughts and as a result we have missed out on the scientifically proven fact that what we actually do is more transformative than what we think.

We've become accustomed in spiritual circles to the idea based on quantum theory that thoughts are vibrational energy waves that impact the invisible energy field of infinite potential that surrounds us. If we get our thought vibrations right we activate limitless power. Focusing on what you want, picturing it in your mind and thinking about it increases the chances of it manifesting in your life. In short, your consciousness creates your world. If you think negative thoughts or focus on your fears, or what you don't want to happen, that is what you will get – but if you reframe your thoughts and focus on your dreams the universe will attract those dreams into your life.

So, perhaps you, along with millions of others, have tried positive thinking and mantras but given up and become disillusioned because your life didn't change for the better.

The positive-thinking theory to change your life sounds too good and too easy to be true, doesn't it? But the thing is you can't *think* your way to a better life – you have to take action. Taking action, doing, is the unlocked door – the obvious way to a better life that we simply have overlooked. But why has it been overlooked? Take a deep breath. Time for some home truths.

**We're not using our brains**: We perhaps misunderstood the positive-thinking mantra. We fall so in love with the idea of thoughts changing our world that we assume thoughts have some magical power to make things happen but if we sat down and (forgive the pun) thought things through we would know that this kind of thing can only happen in *X-Men* movies. In real life we have to take action. Let me give an example: two athletes both dream of success but one of them trains harder and longer than the other and wins Olympic gold. Both believed they would succeed and that self-belief was an essential ingredient but the factor that made all the difference was that the Olympic champion also took the necessary action to ensure victory: he trained harder.

**We're not willing to go the extra mile:** When faced with the challenge of hard work to achieve our goals most of us would far rather take it easy or seek the comfort of the familiar. I'm trying to avoid the word laziness here but it isn't easy. Let me give another example. Ask a child if they want to eat chocolate later or right now and they will choose the now option. It is human nature to go for immediate gratification rather than to delay it for our long-term good.

**We are scared of standing out**: Everybody likes to belong but when we start to become someone who is disciplined and focused toward positive change the chances are that we might lose friends. If the people in our life feel lost or confused but aren't doing anything to resolve that, they may struggle to adapt when they see us pulling ourselves together. That well-worn phrase 'misery loves company' springs to mind. It takes courage to stand out from the crowd and be the best that you can be. This quote from the brilliant Samuel L. Jackson movie *Coach Carter* – which is a film all about the power of action and daily ritual, so thoroughly recommended – says it all:

'Our deepest fear is not that we are inadequate. Our deepest fear is that we are powerful beyond measure. It is our light, not our darkness, that most frightens us. Your playing small does not serve the world. There is nothing enlightened about shrinking so that other people won't feel insecure around you. We are all meant to shine as children do. It's not just in some of us; it is in everyone.'

**We can't focus in terms of forever**: It is tough to stay motivated when we think we have to do something forever but if you only think in terms of the next three weeks your mind will more likely get you to commit. Thinking in terms of forever will demotivate. Three weeks is something the mind can work with.

**We get bored**: The most obvious reason why we find change hard is boredom. There are many studies that link the amount of meaning and enjoyment you experience from an activity to the frequency of undertaking that activity.[4, 6] So that is why all the rituals in this book are explained in terms of their spiritual meaning so they resonate deeply with you. Remember, this is a book about life-changing rituals, not life-changing habits. If I was simply urging you to make positive lifestyle changes, I would be talking about incorporating habits into your life that are good for you. Although that is a fine place to start, the chances of long-term success are seriously limited if you don't imbue these activities with meaning. In addition, there is also a strong emphasis on enjoyment in this book. None of the rituals here will bore you because they are so stimulating and the more you do them the more you will learn about yourself – and, let's face it, self-discovery is a topic most of us find endlessly fascinating.

**We haven't switched to automatic yet**: If you have ever learned a musical instrument or trained in a particular sport you will know that it is constant repetition that yields rewards. If you miss a day of practice, you pay the price with poor performance the next day. You have to practise until it becomes second nature and you don't have to think about the technique anymore but about the performance or your winning strategy – this is called unconscious competence. It is the same with committing yourself to daily rituals. You can't give yourself a day off; they need to become a part of your life so that over time they lead to accuracy of performance or realization of your life goals. You should start seeing the positive benefits around the three-week mark so at that point you are far more likely to make these changes forever because you have noticed the positive benefits. At this point too your rituals will have become second nature. In a nutshell, you can't imagine a day of your life without them.


## PRELIMINARIES

'There is a ritual looking for us.'

Shaman ritual


The 21 rituals in this book are ones that I have gathered from the extensive research I have done on habits and the power of rituals to change lives for the better.

Please remember though that it is not the ritual that matters but the personal meaning you assign to it. You don't have to even believe in your ritual but you do need to make it personal, so use the ones given in this book as your starting point. Understand the meaning behind it and the reason you are doing it (all this will be explained for each ritual) and then find a way to make it uniquely yours. For example, play around with the wording if affirmations are involved so they speak to you more. If, however, you prefer to keep strictly to my recommendations for performing a ritual that is fine too, as long as you have made the choice to embrace it. What matters most is that each ritual feels easy and natural and is simple to add into your day. If you feel uncomfortable or silly modify things until it feels right for you. For example, if you aren't keen on writing a journal, record yourself talking on your mobile instead.

You don't need incense, candles or other equipment to perform the rituals in this book. You also don't need to do any preliminary reading or preparation, or to block out time from your busy life, as these rituals take no more than a few moments each, or minutes each day in total, to perform. All you need is an open mind that is willing to change old routines and approach each day in a different way or see your world in a new perspective, and a heart that knows what is good for you.

Of course, you can pick and choose which rituals to incorporate into your life but for maximum impact and for the most powerful transformation to occur, I highly recommend doing all 21 every day.

At the start of each bright new day during this 21-day period tell yourself that you are going to try something new and then in the days ahead become an observer of your own life. Look for evidence of positive change and don't give up until you find it. If you went online to buy something you wouldn't give up until you found it, so apply the same determination to your daily life here. Be prepared for days when things feel harder or tougher to accomplish or you get it wrong or don't see results. Remember, the road to success is paved with failure and it took Edison 1,000 failed attempts to perfect the light bulb. You don't need to keep going for 1,000 days – just enough to kick start positive transformation in all areas of your life.

My recommendation is to mark a date in your calendar to begin – preferably tomorrow – and start as soon as you wake up with the morning rituals, then the afternoon ones in the afternoon and the evening rituals in the evening. You will also find that because they feel so natural they are extremely easy to remember and incorporate into your life. Most important, as we all lead busy lives these days, they are not time consuming.

You'll notice that some of the rituals require more information and advice than others but, regardless of the length of the discussion, they are all simple and easy and can all be performed in a matter of moments.

'Ritual is necessary for us to know anything.'

Ken Kesey

## TERMS AND CONDITIONS

Only one term – you must perform all 21 of the rituals every day without fail for 21 days. If you forget a day you need to restart at day one. There is no exception to this because it takes your brain at least 21 days to rewire and accept a new ritual (see page xvi). The success of this book is measured by your ability to stick with all the 21 rituals for 21 consecutive days so it becomes second nature to you.

# WHAT TO EXPECT

'Ritual is a more effective means than law to achieve order.'
Jonathan Chan

Day one won't be a problem because everything is new and you will be eager to move ahead and have a go. This honeymoon period will last a few days. Around day four is when you are likely to face challenges. There is wisdom in the saying 'Old habits die hard' because right about this time you may experience all kinds of resistance to pull you back to the way things were. I can't stress how important it is at this stage to stay strong.

Around the end of week two you will start to enter the stage of flow – when the rituals feel more like a natural and an easy part of your life. Life before your rituals may start to feel distant and you may already have started to feel some of the benefits.

Give yourself a big pat on the back if you have got close to the end of week two because you are already well on your way to fully integrating the rituals into your life and hitting that all important symbolic 21-day mark.

At the end of each ritual, you'll find 'For the record' – this is your reminder to write down in your journal the benefits of the ritual and what you have observed throughout the day: how it has brought the sacred into your life and any positive changes to your life.

## YOUR INVITATION

'Life is a ritual of love and union.'

Vishwas Chavan

Finally, I would like to take this opportunity to invite you to prove to me the effectiveness of these 21 life-changing rituals to transform your life for the better. Please do get in touch with me as I welcome all your feedback after you have completed the 21 days. See page 194 for details on how to get in touch with me.

OK, ready to being your three-week journey to a happier and more successful life? Let's jump right in and wake up with determination first...

# PART I

# WAKE WITH DETERMINATION
# 7 LIFE-CHANGING MORNING RITUALS

'You've got to wake up each morning with determination if you are to retire to bed with satisfaction.'

George Lormier

All seven of the rituals here should be performed every morning for the next 21 days as soon as you get up and before you begin your work, school or daily schedule. I'm going to call this time, when most of us normally get dressed and have breakfast and rush around getting ready for the day ahead, your 'power time' because what you do in that time will set the tone for the rest of the day.

When was the last time you were genuinely excited about getting up and leapt out of bed on purpose, keen to start your day? Perhaps it was on your birthday or wedding day? Perhaps it was because you had to catch a plane or start a new job? Or perhaps it was way back when you were a child and it was Christmas morning?

Whatever the reasons you were excited to wake up, I want you to remember how it felt to wake up with energy and a genuine desire to enjoy every minute of the day ahead. This book is really all about re-creating that experience of waking up feeling amazing, eager to start the day and live a life on purpose for the rest of your life.

# LIFE-CHANGING RITUAL #1

# WAKE UP EARLIER

'I never knew a man come to greatness or eminence who lay abed late in the morning.'

Jonathan Swift

Several recent studies from the University of Toronto published in the *Harvard Business Review* confirm that there is a correlation between rising early and reaching your dreams in life.[1] There are exceptions, of course, but people who get up earlier are healthier, happier, slimmer, more positive and generally more successful in life and work than those who choose to lie in. Energy, positivity and discipline are required to get up early day in day out and these are the qualities that great achievers share.

In other words, productive and successful people don't lie in. Waking up early is a sacred ritual for them and many have openly stated that it is the key to their success in life. If you find it hard to get up in the mornings taking control of your waking schedule will be a shock to the system but it might just be what you need to kick start positive change.

First, though, it is important that you understand the benefits of rising early so you can make waking up in the morning an activity filled with personal meaning and importance – in other words, you ritualize it.

## THE BENEFITS

'Early to bed and early to rise makes a man healthy, wealthy and wise.'

Benjamin Franklin

So what are the benefits of early rising? A lot of them are obvious but still worth stating:

**One step ahead:** If you were in a race getting a head start could determine whether you win or lose. When you wake up early you begin your day before most people, and that puts you a step ahead and gives you a psychological boost from the moment you rise. So, if your alarm goes off and a voice tells you just five more minutes won't hurt, ignore it and remind yourself that staying in bed puts you at a disadvantage. If you can take charge of that inner voice first thing there will be no stopping, as you'll have a winner's mind-set.

**Productivity will soar:** Knowing that you are ahead of the game will motivate you and that motivation will lead to increased productivity throughout the day. You will also have more time to get done what needs to be done.

**Taking control:** Getting a head start gives you the quiet time you need to plan your day and manage your goals and activities effectively. This makes you feel disciplined, organized and in control of your day rather than your day controlling you.

**Peace and quiet:** The early morning hours are beautiful mostly because they are often so quiet and peaceful. (You'll be hearing more about the importance of peace and quiet for focus.)

**Time for food and exercise:** If you rise early you are more likely to eat a healthy breakfast, which research shows is the most beneficial meal of the day for optimum mental and physical health.[2] And if you do some exercise first thing this sets you up for the day with even more energy and focus. You will feel invincible.

**Optimum creativity:** Many early risers say that they do their best thinking and creative work first thing when they wake up. So if you have always longed to write a novel follow in the footsteps of giants such as Ernest Hemingway, a famous early riser, and use that time to start writing or doing whatever creative task inspires you.

## ANECDOTAL EVIDENCE

'Think in the morning.'

William Blake

I used to be the kind of person who never had a problem sleeping – indeed I could literally fall asleep anywhere, like a baby. In my twenties when I wasn't rushing about with work and didn't have any commitments, I could easily spend an entire day in bed. My problem wasn't sleeping – it was waking up. I would only wake up and force myself out of bed if I absolutely had to. Even when I had to wake for work or anything else, I would rush around in a panic and barely get to where I needed to be on time. I was one of those always-five-or-ten-minutes'-late kind of person.

There were, however, odd occasions when I would wake up at about 4 or 5 a.m. wide-eyed and full of energy. I'd get up and have an amazing morning where I prepared myself properly for the day ahead and gathered my thoughts but these mornings were all too rare. The night before, I would think about setting my alarm earlier so I could have another stress-free morning and productive day as a result, but my lazy self never let me do it and even if I did set my alarm early and I was still feeling sleepy when it woke me I'd just go back to sleep. However, once I had researched and read countless testimonials about the serious benefits of getting up earlier I made the decision to give early rising a proper try. I knew I needed a method that would be impossible for me to ignore. I needed a wake-up-earlier ritual that would be difficult, if not impossible, for me to ignore however groggy I felt.

What did I come up with? I told myself when my alarm clock went off that if I didn't get up immediately my day would not be as productive as it could potentially be. The success of my day depended on me getting up right now. Sounds pretty irrational but for me this method works because I can be a bit superstitious. I don't walk under ladders, for example. In my mind I tell myself that not getting up early is a bad-luck magnet. I tell my mind that every morning and it works without fail. Of course, this method may not work for you. You may prefer to do what one of my friends does. Warning: it's pretty drastic. She writes an email and schedules it to go out at 7 a.m. The email tells everyone that it has gone out because she is still asleep and anyone who replies to her will receive £1. She has a large mailing list so the fear of monetary loss as a result of sleeping in gets her up on time every morning. She then needs to reschedule the email for the following morning!

Now that's a pretty dramatic way to make yourself get up but it has had a 100 per cent success rate for my friend. I think a much more effective (and potentially less expensive way) is simply to place your alarm clock at the other side of the room so you can't be tempted to hit the snooze button. When buying an alarm clock buy one that doesn't fill you with a sense of dread when you hear it. You might also want to invest in a natural-daylight wake-up lamp, as they can be especially beneficial for cold winter mornings.

For me personally, the radio or some music playing is preferable to a traditional sounding alarm. Whatever you decide, be sure that it is not something that irritates you every morning. You want your early start to the day to be as positive as possible.

As soon as I got into the routine of waking up earlier my days and my life transformed for the better. I felt calmer and more in control, and was no longer rushing about feeling like a late arrival. I started my wake-up-early ritual in my late-thirties after having my two children. I knew I had to do something drastic because my life was chaos. I was getting writing assignments but missing deadlines. I kept trying to carve out some alone time but, of course, with two young children that was so hard. However, when I got up two hours earlier I gave myself the gift of that time. It was in those magic early morning hours that I wrote my first *Sunday Times* top 10 bestseller. I had written and ghost-written many books prior to that and they had sold reasonably well but this was my first stand-out book. I truly believe getting up earlier and writing in those magical quiet hours was the miracle ingredient for success.

From that moment on – with the odd exception when my alarm breaks down, I'm ill or on holiday – I have woken up early. I have done that for so many years now that it is very hard for me to have a lie-in and if people urge me to treat myself, I have to tell them that for me it isn't a treat. It just gives me a headache. I have to get up! If I don't my day won't be a great one – and I want every day of my life to be a great one!

## ROADBLOCKS

'An early morning walk is a blessing for the whole day.'
Henry Thoreau

There are as many reasons for not wanting to get up in the morning as there are different people, but here are some very common ones:

**I'm not a morning person:** You have always enjoyed working late into the night. OK, if that's the case give the wake-up ritual a try and then discard it if it doesn't make you feel and work better. Also, you don't necessarily have to get up at 5 a.m. if you went to bed at 2 a.m. and normally get up at 9 a.m. If that is your lifestyle, get up at 7 a.m., as that would be early rising for you and in your world you will still be two hours ahead of yourself than before. In addition, research from Harvard has shown that night owls can reset their body clocks or circadian rhythm by going outside into daylight earlier in the morning.[3]

**Motivation:** If you don't want to get up early because you haven't got enough to do then fill your day with to-dos. There are so many exciting and wonderful things to do in this life there really is no excuse for saying I haven't got anything to do. Schedule appointments, even non-essential ones, like a haircut or breakfast with a friend, early so you have to get up.

**Can't wake up:** If you always wake up feeling groggy and find it impossible to resist the snooze button, as suggested earlier put your alarm clock on the other side of your room so you have to get up to turn it off. Find your own way to 'threaten' or force yourself to get out of bed.

**I need my sleep:** We all need quality sleep but we actually don't need as much as we think we need. Studies on sleep show that around six to eight hours is optimum for most of us.[4] You don't really need more than that unless you have a medical condition. If you are worried you will be sleep deprived go to bed an hour or two earlier. To give your body time to adjust to lighter sleeping hours if you are used to getting lots of sleep gently ease into the wake-up-early ritual. Don't set your alarm for 5 a.m. if you normally get up at 7.30 a.m. Set your alarm for 15 minutes earlier and then when you have eased into that earlier waking time set it half an hour or an hour earlier until you hit your target wake-up-early time. You could even start smaller and wake up five minutes earlier and then add five minutes to that time each day. What matters here is that you are getting into the routine of waking up earlier than you normally do.

**My work schedule makes an early start impossible:** Of course, a late schedule is essential for some occupations, night shifts and lifestyles but getting up earlier than you normally would and giving yourself that power time before your working day starts is still possible.

# PRACTICE:
# HOW TO GET UP EARLY

OK, the alarm has gone off and all you want to do is hit snooze and go back to sleep. Here's a simple technique when the alarm goes off: take a deep breath and contented stretch and say out loud the words, 'Wake up now.' Then roll over and put both your feet on the ground. Then take a deep breath again before standing up and stretching again. You may find it a bit strange to talk out loud to yourself in this way but trust me it really can work.

The reason we find it hard to get up is that it isn't easy to leave the feeling of being cosy and warm so the temptation is always strong to linger in bed, but remind yourself that getting up earlier sets the tone for your whole day.

## BRINGING THE RITUAL TO LIFE

'The reason I like having a morning routine is that not only does it instil a sense of purpose, peace and ritual to my day, but it ensures that I'm getting certain things done in the morning – namely, my goals.'

Leo Babauta

Whether you are a morning person or a night owl the prospect of leaping out of bed earlier is not one to be relished. To make sure you don't go to bed with good intentions of waking up earlier but then when morning comes the lure of the snooze button is too strong, it is vital to establish a morning wake-up ritual that has significance which is deeply personal and meaningful to you.

When you wake up treat getting out of bed immediately as a ritual – a key element for your success in life. Congratulate yourself and celebrate the fact that you have taken this important step. Fill your waking-up moments with deep meaning.

The reason I am asking you to do this is that when we wake up we may be awake in body but not in mind and one powerful way to wake up your mind is to fill it with meaning. Then once you are on your feet create your own early-morning routine. This adds structure and provides a consistent and strong foundation to your day. It doesn't matter in what order you do things. The important things is that what you do is written in stone, it remains the same each day for the next 21 days and that you understand how important this routine is for you to have a successful day. It is your morning wake-up ritual, after all, so treat it with all the reverence and respect it deserves.

Here's a suggested ritual, but I encourage you to create your own routine.

Wake up at 6 a.m. and celebrate the new day perhaps by repeating an affirmation or mantra, such as 'Choose happy' or 'I can do it', a few times. Get out of bed and stretch. Shower and dress. Have a healthy breakfast so you don't end up reaching for a sugar fix later, by avoiding sugar and caffeine – as both cause blood sugar swings and can result in an energy dip – and including protein to balance blood sugar levels and provide sustained energy.

# FOR THE RECORD

**Life-changing ritual:** Wake up earlier.

**The theory:** This will give you a head start and improve the quality of your day.

**The practice:** Write down at the end of each day how more productive your day has been and compare that with how correctly you observed the details of your sacred morning ritual. See if there is a correlation.

## STAYING MOTIVATED

'He that would thrive must rise at five.'

Proverb

Until you try waking up early for 21 days to give your body and mind a chance to fully adjust to the new routine you can't really know for sure if waking up early is going to change your life for the better. In other words, you have the motivation now to get up early. You are testing a theory. Remember, if you don't see the benefits after 21 days you can discard it, but, given all the reported positives that research associates with early rising, you really owe it to yourself to at the very least give it a try.

There will be roadblocks to work through but the important thing is not to stop. Even getting up 10 minutes earlier than you normally would takes you in the right direction. If you do lie in one day you will need to restart at day one of your 21-day programme again but that isn't a disaster. There is absolutely nothing wrong with doing that. In fact, restarting at day one will give you even more motivation and incentive to prove to yourself you have the discipline to see this through for the next three weeks.

## ON YOUR FEET

'It's mind over mattress.'

Robin Sharma

Waking up earlier gives you a head start and the energy, motivation and focus to create the life you have always wanted. And for a final incentive to throw back those bedcovers here are some famous early risers.

Robin Sharma is a world-famous personal-development guru and author of the million-selling *The Monk Who Sold His Ferrari*. He is an early riser himself and noticed that an early-rising ritual is a crucial success factor of high achievers the world over.

John Grisham's crime thriller novels have electrified the world. He rises at 5 a.m. every morning to create his masterpieces.

Margaret Thatcher, the 'Iron Lady', famously got up at 5 a.m. without fail.

Richard Branson, founder and chairman of the Virgin group, wakes at about 5.45 in the morning even when relaxing at his private island, deliberately leaving the curtains open so the sun wakes him.

Other 5 a.m., or earlier, risers include: the Obamas, Apple CEO Tim Cook, Pepsico CEO Indra Nooyi, Mark Wahlberg, Starbucks CEO Howard Schultz, Anna Wintour, Peter the Great, Christopher Columbus, George Washington, Thomas Jefferson; the list of powerful and successful people who rise early could go on forever as it is such a common theme.

## DO IT: WAKE UP EARLY!

So, start creating the ritual of rising early from tomorrow. It will take a while to adjust and you won't feel super-focused, energetic and creative right away but stick with it for 21 days and test the theory. Millions of super-successful people simply can't have got it wrong.

'Every morning you have two choices – continue to sleep with dreams or wake up and chase your dreams. The choice is yours.'

Anonymous

# LIFE-CHANGING RITUAL #2

# STRETCH INSTEAD OF REACHING FOR YOUR PHONE

'I wake up every morning and I surprise myself. I wake up to a new me.'

Gina Carano

We've all done it. I know I have. The alarm goes off and as soon as we are awake enough the first thing we do is clumsily reach for our mobile to check to see if there is anything urgent. Today, even those who aren't particularly drawn to technology tend to check their phones first thing for messages, texts, emails, updates and so on. Over 60 per cent of smartphone users say they charge their phones on their bedside table so they can easily find it first thing in the morning when they wake up.[1]

Ritual #2 asks you NOT to do that and take a big lazy stretch instead.

## THE BENEFITS

'I've learned to love myself because I sleep with myself every night and I wake up with myself every morning.'

Gabourey Sidibe

If the first thing you do when you wake up is reach for your phone, the signal you are sending your brain is that the needs of others – the messages on your phone – are more important than your own needs. This simple action will dictate your whole day. It is crucial that you put yourself centre stage in those first few waking moments of the day. Acknowledge your own importance and your own needs first and foremost. This isn't selfish. In fact, it is the most unselfish thing you can do because you can't give to others what you don't already have yourself.

Checking your phone first thing will dampen the tone for the whole day. Replacing that with a glorious arm or whole body stretch and yawn is something that feels good just for you. Not only does this help both mind and body wake up, it is a signal to both yourself, and the universe, that you are acknowledging your needs and for the risk of repeating what has now become an advertising cliché, you are worth all the blessings the universe can send you.

This ritual sounds so very simple but it truly isn't all that easy. Mobile phone addiction is a growing cause for concern these days and if you are checking your phone first thing every morning you are edging closer to becoming unhealthily dependent on technology. Some people are so attached to their phones they go into meltdown when their phone breaks or they lose it. It is as if they can't function.

A recent report suggests that the average Briton checks their phones a staggering 50 times or more a day and in the US researchers have even established a 20-point questionnaire to find out how addicted people are to their phones.[2] Phone addiction is becoming increasingly common and it is as damaging to your life as alcohol or gambling.[3] In addition, studies have shown that sleeping near electronic devices can hinder sleep and sleep experts advise leaving gadgets powered off or in another room.[4] I'm not suggesting that you stop using your phone (that's impossible in this day and age) but that you downgrade your phone's importance in your life. A phone should never become more important to you than your own wellbeing so this ritual is truly putting you centre stage. It requires you not to go to bed with your phone and certainly not to wake up with it.

Replacing reaching for your phone with an enormous stretch and a giant yawn has the obvious benefit of feeling really good and can also help you wake up. Research shows stretching increases flexibility, relieves any tension and improves circulation. In short, stretching is the perfect way to greet the day.[5]

## ANECDOTAL EVIDENCE

'The best way to make your dreams come true is to wake up.'
Paul Valery

After a lifetime of very light phone use up to a few years ago, I was suddenly in touch for work-related reasons with someone, let's call him Dave, who came up with an idea to market my books online that I hadn't thought of before. Dave communicated with me only through texts and messages and, after initial reluctance, I suddenly found myself deep in the world of 21$^{st}$-century technology. Prior to that I had felt email was pretty exciting but now I was truly at the cutting edge. I'm incredibly grateful for that electric shock, as it helped me overcome my allergy to all things online and I now love working on my author page on Facebook because it allows me to form a more immediate connection with my readers. However, Dave was also someone who always seemed to be texting or online and within a matter of weeks, as we worked on a business plan, I was drawn into this online world. At first it felt incredibly exciting but then it started to feel like a burden.

Some nights I would sleep with my phone clutched in my hand because I was afraid I might miss an important message and set back the business plan. Dave was never offline. It was as if he never slept and whenever I went online he was suddenly there, watching and waiting. I felt I needed to be constantly vigilant like he was too.

Friends and family started to get used to me having my head buried in my laptop or my phone – which had previously been blissfully silent most of the time and was now suddenly beeping constantly. I lived in this state of permanent online readiness for a year and the irony is that that year was the most unproductive year of my life to date. Not only did the so-called business plan not work out and my writing slowed to a halt, but I also lost friends and upset loved ones because my thoughts were always wrapped up in my phone when we met up. Eventually, even I began to see that I was getting addicted to my phone and I had to start to wean myself off it and get back to doing what I loved best – spending time with loved ones and writing. The problem was my phone had become such a huge part of my life I didn't know how to go offline. Fortunately, the universe stepped in. I lost my phone.

I remember the absolute panic that hit me when I searched my bag and couldn't find my phone. I had used it last in a coffee bar so I rushed back there but the bar was closed. I actually began to sweat and completely forgot that I had to pick my daughter up from a school event, so overwhelming was my reaction to the loss of my phone. Eventually, I remembered and asked a friend to call my daughter to let her know I was on my way; however, with my focus still on my phone I felt as if I had lost an arm or a leg. I freaked out! It was then that my wise and wonderful friend looked at me and said, 'You know, it's just a phone. You can get another with the same number. You have totally lost perspective, Theresa.' Only then did I realize how insane this had all become. It took physical separation from my phone, however, to truly drive the point home. As long as my phone was still by my side it was casting its spell.

I went home that evening feeling more ashamed than anxious about my phone and as the evening wore on and I realized that there were other ways to contact the people that mattered to me I felt calmer and calmer. I also actually spoke to people for the first time in months rather than messaging them and it felt right. I had a terrific night's sleep and in the morning the bliss of knowing I couldn't reach for my phone and it couldn't hold me hostage anymore was incredible. Getting up didn't feel like a stressful chore but a pleasure.

Later that morning I went to the coffee shop and found that a kind person had handed my phone in. Having it back in my hand again, it felt like a stranger or an unwelcome guest. It took me a good few hours to switch it on properly and look at my messages. Of course, there were dozens but as

I scrolled through them I realized that not one of them was essential, and how much time I would have wasted reading and replying to them.

From that moment on I have never let my phone take over my life in the same way again. I always place it in another room at night and have told my family and friends that if anything is urgent they need to call me rather than text or message me, as I have limited time now for texts and online contact.

The most wonderful thing about this new development is that since then I have been a hundred times more productive and happy not just in my work and writing but in every area of my life.


## ROADBLOCKS

'The sun is new each day.'

Heraclitus


As with any new way of doing things there are going to be roadblocks but in the case of this ritual there really is only one: What if I miss something really urgent?

That was exactly my reaction when I lost my phone but it proved to be totally flawed. If someone sends you a message or a text and you don't reply instantly it does not mean they will lose interest or you will miss out, in fact quite the opposite. If you are replying instantly it suggests first that you aren't that busy and second that you are not fully involved with your work or life. This doesn't mean you should not reply to people when messages come in – of course you should – but you should reply in your own good time and when convenient to you. If it happens that you have the time to reply right away go ahead and do it, but if not then the message can wait for a reply until you are ready to give it. This is all about putting yourself, your life and work centre stage, as that is the secret of attracting success. If you are constantly running around assisting or responding to others you dissipate your energy and the universe can't build a connection with you because you are all things to all people but not a source of energy yourself.

As for the 'missing something urgent from family and friends' roadblock, unless the situation is extreme like a hostage situation (and let's face it the likelihood of that happening is so extremely rare you can't live your life thinking it might happen), if something is truly urgent they will *call* you rather than send a text, email or message.

And, finally, if you are constantly answering texts and messages because you are worried people won't stay in your life or like you if you don't reply, or won't want to work with you if you don't give instant responses, then the issue here is not your phone use but your serious lack of self-esteem. I hope this ritual will be a starting point for you to realize that if people only like you because you are always available and respond to them when they want then they are not the kind of people you deserve in your life. You deserve people who value you, not what you can give them. Better to have only a few authentic friends than hundreds who don't see your true value. A true friend will understand and respect your need for personal space and be happy to hear from you when you can and not when they demand.

Seen in this light all the rituals in this book can help you build that essential foundation stone for a happier and more successful life – self-esteem. Do them every day and they will help you focus more on your needs and what makes you happy. As you practise them and your self-worth grows, the law of attraction will start to attract good things into your life and when you enjoy your glorious early morning stretch think of it as recognizing your own value and believing you are worthy of every happiness.

## PRACTICE: HOW TO STRETCH

You would think it would be the simplest thing in the world to stretch instead of reaching for your phone but it is a little harder if you are used to phone checking first thing in the morning and needs a bit of planning. The best advice is to stop charging your phone on your bedside table and to never use it as an alarm clock. Invest in a simple, old-fashioned alarm clock and keep your phone charging in another room when you go to sleep – so you are not tempted to reach out for it.

Then in the morning when your alarm goes either do a big arm and body stretch and accompanying yawn while lying in bed or when you stand up. Better still do both: stretch in bed and then again when you stand up.

## BRINGING THE RITUAL TO LIFE

'When you arise in the morning, think of what a precious privilege it is to be alive – to breathe, to think, to enjoy, to love.'

Marcus Aurelius

You may wonder how it is possible to ritualize not reaching for your phone and stretching but it couldn't be simpler. With your phone waiting for you in the other room, when you stretch and notice how good it feels see this as a reminder of the importance of acknowledging your own needs. For those few blissful moments don't think about anything except what feels good to you. The world and its demands can wait a few moments. Right now the focus is all on you.

Taking a moment to stretch is adding intention to your day. You are setting the tone for your day ahead and this simple act of doing something just for you may reflect how productive, happy and at peace you feel for the rest of the day. Think of your stretch as a ritual that can give you the power to wake up on the right side of the bed every morning.

## FOR THE RECORD

**Life-changing ritual:** Stretch first thing in the morning and leave your message checking until later.

**The theory:** This will put the focus firmly on your needs first thing in the morning to set the tone for the rest of the day.

**The practice:** Observe how you feel when you simply enjoying stretching in the morning and not starting your day with emails, texts and to-do lists.

## DO IT: STRETCH INSTEAD OF REACHING FOR YOUR PHONE!

If the first physical thing you do in the morning after waking up isn't about you then the chances are the rest of the day will not be centred on you either. In the words of Micah Baldwin, CEO of Graphicly, 'Find something that is yours and yours alone.' Stretching is a powerful act of self-awareness and love that will help ensure an amazing day ahead.

Keep stretching and placing your needs over that of the mobile and you will keep having more and more amazing days and this is when your life truly starts to change for the better.

'I have always been delighted at the prospect of a new day, a fresh try, one more start, with perhaps a bit of magic waiting somewhere behind the morning.'

J.B. Priestley

# LIFE-CHANGING RITUAL #3

# ASK YOURSELF ONE SIMPLE QUESTION

'For the past 33 years, I have looked in the mirror every morning and asked myself: "If today were the last day of my life, would I want to do what I am about to do today?" And whenever the answer has been "No" for too many days in a row, I know I need to change something.'

Steve Jobs

Research from the University of Nottingham and the National Institute of Education in Singapore proves what most of us instinctively know already: will power is strongest in the morning.[1] If you think of your willpower as a muscle, the more you use that muscle the stronger it will get, but it will also get depleted and less effective over time when continually used. In other words, the longer the day goes on, the more fatigue and distractions scatter our focus, so not only does this mean it is important to make your early mornings count but also to start our day with a powerful and determined focus that encourages us to get important tasks done as early as possible.

The third morning ritual is all about ensuring that from the moment you wake up, your powerful and determined focus sets the tone for your morning and, by extension, the rest of your day. The best way to do that is to ask yourself one simple question – one that Steve Jobs made famous:

'If today were the last day of my life, would I want to do what I am about to do today?'

First, though, it is important that you clearly understand why asking this one simple question each morning is so powerful so you can fill it with personal meaning and importance – in other words, you ritualize it.

## THE BENEFITS

'The power to question is the basis of all human progress.'
Indira Gandhi

I'd be truly surprised if you hadn't heard about the power of positive affirmations. You know those 'I can do it' statements or ones like 'I am amazing', 'I am lovable' and so on. Those who incorporate affirmations into their lives testify to their success and even scientific research suggests there may actually be something in this.

According to Dr Joseph Dispenza, author of *Evolve Your Brain*, affirmations, like prayer, may be able to change the brain at a cellular level and your thoughts or beliefs about yourself can impact how you feel and operate.[2] The theory is that neurons in your brain connect to your thoughts and organize themselves into a pattern, and the more you think and feel in a certain way the stronger these patterns become. In time affirmations can break down negative patterns and replace them with positive ones. In science this is called neuroplasticity.

Other research published in *Psychological Science* and the *Journal of the Association for Psychological Science*[3] also shows that affirmations have the power to boost performance and numerous other studies strongly suggest that affirmations really can and do work. So, given all this confirmation from the world of science you may be wondering why I'm not simply suggesting some positive affirmations for Ritual #3. Of course, there are valid reasons and these reasons come not from me but from actual research into how the mind works.[4]

First, questions dictate the way your thoughts move. They are the catalyst and the motivator and when you have a thought it is always in answer to a question. In other words, questions are a higher form of thought than answers because they stimulate brain activity more. Questions also force your mind to focus in a specific direction. In studies on the most successful people in the world a common theme was that they focused their energy on how to achieve their desires, rather than the desire itself. Questions gave them the stimulation, creativity, direction, motivation and momentum to reach for their dreams.

## THE POWER OF A QUESTION

'Don't count the days, make the days count.'

Muhammad Ali

Now you've seen the reasoning behind turning the spotlight on questions rather than affirmations let's focus on the question itself. Why the Steve Jobs one in particular? For one simple reason: it works.

Yes, it is a hypothetical question because if it were actually true most people would simply want to spend their time with loved ones rather than their own lives, but let's imagine you have one final day to do what you really feel passionate about. Now ask yourself if what you are about to do today is what you would want to do with your last day. If the answer is negative then you need to ask yourself why you are not doing work that you love all day. You need to keep asking that question for at least the next 21 days to stimulate your mind into finding creative solutions and a way forward.

## ANECDOTAL EVIDENCE

'Realize deeply that the present moment is all you ever have.'
Eckhart Tolle

As a spiritual author finding anecdotal evidence for the power of ritual was extremely easy, as I just needed to look into my file of near-death-experience stories sent to me by my readers over the years. A strong theme in all this stories, and in the research on them, confirms that after a brush with death people return to their everyday lives with renewed focus and passion. They are acutely aware that every day could well be their last and they don't want to waste a precious moment. Here follows a typical example of the kind of stories sent to me – this one was from Paul, one of my readers:

'You know Theresa I saw incredible things when I crossed over to the other side and was clinically dead. I glimpsed the unconditional love that unites us all and the true meaning and purpose of my life. I met departed loved ones and saw beauty I cannot articulate. Returning to earth I don't have the same spiritual vision and understanding that I had when I was in heaven – I think heaven blocks that out because otherwise we wouldn't want to return to earth – but I have been left with this tremendous sense of purpose and energy. I start every day with such a feeling of excitement and urgency. I never had that before. It is as if I see life in colour now whereas before it was black and white. I take nothing about this beautiful life for granted. I know that each day is a chance for me to seize the moment and if I find myself slipping into acceptance and boredom again I remind myself that today could very well be my last day. Of course, there are people who will say my near death experience was all hallucination and I can't prove 100 per cent that they are wrong but what I do know is that almost dying has made me realize with an acuteness I never had before that today could be my last day and because of that I wake up with a desire to make every single day count.'

## ROADBLOCKS

'Enjoy yourself. It's later than you think.'

Chinese proverb

As always, with positive change there are always going to be roadblocks and nowhere is this more the case than with Ritual #3. One that immediately comes to mind is the nagging feeling that it simply isn't realistic to live each day of our life in that heightened state. The need to earn money to support ourselves and those we take care of means that often we simply have to do things that we don't particularly enjoy.

Let's break this down. What the Steve Jobs question requires us to do is not to be reckless but to consider what our actions will be in the day ahead. We are asking ourselves if we are going to do something today that matters and makes a difference to us or if it is just going to be another day. We often get so lost in our daily routines that we lose sight of what matters and if day after day we keep doing what doesn't matter to us then it is a negative way to live, which will not attract success. Asking yourself if today is to be your last day is really asking you how you would approach today differently if you knew that. Would you be doing what you are about to do?

All too often people think of the 'live today as if it were your last' mantra as a licence to be reckless, thoughtless and irresponsible but it is none of these. It is about living the day ahead as if the day truly *matters*.

Here are some tips to help you live each day as if it were your last in a realistic and enjoyable way:

**Do you believe in what you are doing?** Remember, if you can see the meaning and bigger picture behind even boring tasks then what you are doing has meaning. For example, nobody loves housework or commuting long distances for work or meetings but if you love your house and family you see why housework is important and if you find meaning in your work you understand the need for your daily commute.

**Do you love your work?** Of course, we have to earn money to look after our loved ones and ourselves but that does not mean you have to earn your money doing things that have no meaning. Take a look at the world around you and you will see that those earning the highest incomes tend to be those who simply love what they do. There is true power in passion so aim to do at least one task each day that makes you feel good and you can take pleasure in doing well.

**Are you giving your day all you have got?** There is a simple way to make each day count and that is to give every person you meet and every activity you undertake your 100 per cent attention or effort. In other words, be a person who always gives your best. Never give half of what you can do and feel proud of all that you say and do.

**Do you know the difference between being busy and doing what is important?** Increasingly today we all live busy lives but try to ensure that you are doing what matters and not just keeping busy.

**Are you putting off your dreams?** Making each day count is not about throwing caution to the wind and chasing long lost dreams but putting steps in place that can take you closer toward realizing some of those dreams and passions. I used to work in a hospice and many of the elderly residents there had the same piece of advice for me: don't put things off, thinking you have time, because suddenly you will wake up one morning and it will be too late. In other words, stop putting off what you have always been meaning to do.

**Are you expressing yourself honestly?** Give others in your life the gift of your truth. Tell others (politely, of course) the truth and be truthful to yourself as well. Tell those you care about deeply that you love them while you still can. One of the most poignant things I read about the 9/11 passengers on the hijacked planes was their final phone calls to loved ones when they knew they were not going to survive. In the great majority of cases these people didn't talk about the terrorists or the injustice or hatred. All their energy and focus was directed towards telling the people they cared about how much they loved them. Their final messages were entirely ones of love. Their last meaning was love.

**Are you enjoying yourself?** There should be enjoyment of some kind in your day. You have this time now on this beautiful earth so use it well. Do something meaningful, even if it is just spending more time with your children or starting the novel you have always wanted to write or pottering in the garden or walking in the park. It does not matter what day of the year it is, or what the weather is like or what you have to do today, always try to enjoy what you do. Remember, a today that isn't quite perfect is always better than a tomorrow that doesn't exist.

# PRACTICE:
# HOW TO ASK THE QUESTION

The simplest and most effective way to incorporate the Steve Jobs question into your life is to ask it first thing in the morning as soon as you wake up after having a good stretch. Once you are up and moving, or better still as soon as your feet touch the ground, make this the first question you ask yourself each day. You can ask it silently with your thoughts but I always find it is much more effective for me to say it out loud.

Try it. Say out loud when you wake up, 'If today were the last day of my life would I want to do what I'm about to do today?'

See how saying something so powerful like that makes you feel.

## BRINGING THE RITUAL TO LIFE

'Live each day as if it were going to be your last; for one day you're sure to be right.'

Harry Harbord Morant

When you ask yourself this question remind yourself that change does not happen over time or within the next year. It happens as soon as we commit to making a change. Many of us spend a lot of our lives hoping things will get better but not actually doing anything about it. It is as if we watch our lives to 'see what happens' but don't actually take control of it.

So, to turn this question into a ritual that can change your life simply fill it with great meaning. Remind yourself that the moment you ask yourself this powerful question and decide and fully commit to making changes by living every day as if it is your last is the moment when things start to actually change.

## FOR THE RECORD

**Life-changing ritual:** Ask the Steve Jobs question.

**The theory:** This will energize your brain and encourage you to find meaning in your day.

**The practice:** Start to notice how this question changes your perspective and thoughts throughout the day. Does your productivity improve when you ask yourself this question in the morning? Does it give rise to further questions about how you're spending your life? Make sure you take a note of any observations in your journal.

### DO IT: ASK YOURSELF ONE SIMPLE QUESTION!

One simple life-changing question: 'If today were your last day, would you want to do what you are doing today?'

Your day is what you decide to make of it. Ask yourself this question again tomorrow and for a minimum of 21 days and potentially every day after that.

What are you waiting for? Start right now. Make your day count.

'Your time is limited. Don't waste it living somebody else's life.'

Steve Jobs

# LIFE-CHANGING RITUAL #**4**

# JUST BREATHE

'If you know the art of breathing you have the strength, wisdom and courage of ten tigers.'

Chinese adage

How about taking a long and satisfying deep breath right now to remind you how great it feels? It doesn't matter what time of day it is try taking a deep breath now. Feels wonderful, doesn't it? If it feels this good now just imagine how energizing and empowering it will feel after your rituals of waking up earlier, stretching and thinking about filling your new day with meaning.

## THE BENEFITS

'Shallow breathing is the root of all evil but conscious deep breathing restores and secures out souls.'

Desmond Green

Study after study has repeatedly shown that deep breathing can make us feel happier, relieve stress, and boost health, energy levels and immunity.[1] The happier and healthier you are the more likely you are to be productive and attract success into your life. The great majority of us lead busy lives and tend to breathe very lightly or shallowly, but making a conscious decision to focus on deep breathing first thing in the morning encourages us to breathe deeper without having to think too much about it.

The benefits of deep breathing are so astonishing entire books have been written on it. Often yogic breathing techniques and complicated names are referenced but in essence what is being referred to here is simply slow, deep breathing. It improves heath and prevents disease by increasing oxygen supply and removing carbon dioxide and other toxins from the body. It encourages better sleep, lowers blood pressure, improves our nervous system and increases circulation. It is great for weight control as the extra oxygen encourages fat burning and because increased blood flow improves digestion. According to the American Medical Student Association it increases energy and stamina and cardiovascular (aerobic) energy.[2-3] Other benefits include pain and stress relief and an increase in happiness because when you breathe deep you release endorphins, the feel-good chemicals in the body. Last, but by no means least, it encourages a good posture because when you breathe deep you tend to stand or sit up straight and the benefits of good posture for general health and for presenting a confident image to the world are well recorded.

Given all these astonishing health benefits and the fact that deep breathing is easy, can be done anywhere and is completely free, it simply doesn't make sense for an intelligent person who wants their life to change for the better in every way not to take a few moments to incorporate it into their daily routine.

## ANECDOTAL EVIDENCE

'You don't need a plan, sometimes you just need to breathe,
trust and let go and see what happens.'

Mandy Hale

Five years ago I kept getting a series of chronically bad
headaches. I went to the doctor and they referred me to an
eye specialist who told me they could find nothing wrong
and I should cut down on the time I spent working on
my computer, as this was straining my eyes and perhaps
triggering my headaches. I did cut down my screen time and
it helped a little but some days I was still relying on painkillers
to get through the day.

Eventually I decided to try the alternative approach
and I went to a holistic doctor trained in both Eastern and
Western medical techniques. We discussed my headaches
and my lifestyle and general health, and instead of getting
a prescription as I expected he simply told me that I was
stressed and had forgotten how to breathe correctly. He said
shallow breathing from my chest rather than my abdomen
was probably restricting blood flow, destroying my posture
and causing my headaches.

I was dumbfounded. Was there a right and wrong way to
breathe? I had seriously never even thought about the way I
breathe. He handed me a leaflet and told me to come back in
a few weeks if my headaches had not gone away.

With no other approach working I decided I had nothing
to lose but give it a try, and so every morning and evening I
did some deep and slow breathing. During that time I started
to notice how I breathed and also started to notice how
others breathed and realized that I was not alone in breathing

incorrectly. I noticed that almost everyone I knew, including myself, breathed from the chest and not from the abdomen, which is far more beneficial to health and wellbeing.

I also realized that one of the characteristics of breathing is that it is something we do without thinking about doing it but it is also something that we can control voluntarily, in the same way we control our limbs. Most of us lead busy lives and the tendency is to breathe shallowly and when we do that it encourages our bodies to feel even more stress and release stress hormones. However, deep breathing triggers the relaxation response so by paying attention to our breathing we can actually control our stress levels.

It was a revelation to learn all this and I changed my breathing accordingly by putting the focus on breathing from my stomach and not my chest. Within 16 days my headaches had completely disappeared and they have not returned since.

It was so incredibly simple. All I needed to do was learn to breathe.

## ROADBLOCKS

'So take a deep breath, pick yourself up, dust yourself off, and start all over again.'                                    Frank Sinatra

There aren't any roadblocks. We all have to breathe – so just take a few moments every morning after you wake up to breathe deeper. If you feel faintly ridiculous standing still taking deep breaths, do it while you engage in other activities or are going about your morning routine. There truly is no reason why anyone can't take long and deep breathes every now and again, unless a medical condition prevents it.

Keep breathing correctly until it becomes a part of your life. You will notice a difference. If you think spending a few moments breathing is vain or you haven't got time because your children or family or friends demand all your attention and focus, remember, if you can't take care of yourself then you can't take care of others. There is a very good reason why when you have a safety brief on a plane they tell you to put on your own breathing mask before helping your children and loved ones.

# PRACTICE:
## HOW TO BREATHE CORRECTLY

You would think this would be simple as breathing is something we continuously do but most of us simply don't do it right. To see if you are breathing right, stop reading and pay attention to your breathing right now. If you can't hear or see anything moving you are breathing shallowly.

To breathe deeply and properly you need to breathe slowly and deeply from your stomach and not from your lungs. You also need to breathe in through your nose and out through your mouth. Each breath in and out should be around three seconds. When you breathe in slowly from your stomach through your nose allow your lungs to fill completely with air. Then when your lungs feel full hold for a second or two and then exhale slowly and push all the air out of your lungs through your mouth.

> The breath is coming from your stomach (abdomen) so as you do this you should see your stomach expand rather than your chest. Babies breathe in this way so it should come naturally to you with a little practice.

## BRINGING THE RITUAL TO LIFE

'For breath is life and if you breathe well you will live long on earth.'

Sanskrit proverb

My suggestion is to take 5–10 deep breaths each morning when you get up. You could also repeat this ritual in the evening. If you are always rushed in the morning put a sticky note up on your bathroom mirror with the word 'breathe'.

Spending a few moments each morning consciously breathing slowly and deeply so that you bring oxygen deep down into your lungs is a simple way to energize your day. It will also help bring focus. Knowing all the benefits of deep breathing will make it easy for you to ritualize the activity and fill it with deep meaning. This exercise might also help:

As you take your 5–10 deep breaths, visualize your lungs expelling toxins as grey or waste as you exhale and your lungs expanding with sacred or golden-light sunshine energy when you inhale. Remember shallow breathing only fills a small portion of your lungs but your bodily organs and systems, including your brain, can function so much better when you fill your lungs fully and bring oxygen into your body to cleanse and energize it.

# FOR THE RECORD

**Life-changing ritual:** Take 10 deep breaths every morning.

**The theory:** This will invigorate your brain and body and ease stress, helping you focus on what you want to achieve in the day.

**The practice:** Notice how you feel after taking a deep breath and, in particular, how it helps to release tension from your body and mind. Any time during the day, when you notice tension or stress creeping in, pause and take a deep breath and release. Is there a correlation between remembering to pay attention to your breathing and your motivation levels as you progress through your day and the following days – take a note of any observations.

## DO IT: JUST BREATHE!

Breathing is non-negotiable – it is something you have to do so you may as well do it well. Keep doing a few moments of deep breathing every morning and it will become a habit so you do it without thinking and feel happier and healthier as a result. Ritualize that habit by reminding yourself every time you do your morning breathing routine that this is about so much more than breathing – it is about transforming your life for the better in every possible way.

Nothing could be simpler or more natural... Just breathe...

'When you own your breath, nobody can steal your peace.'
Unknown

# LIFE-CHANGING RITUAL #5

# SMILE IN THE MIRROR

'Smile in the mirror. Do that every morning and you'll start to see a big difference in your life.'

Yoko Ono

'You are never fully dressed without a smile' is how the saying goes and morning Ritual #5 completely agrees. We often think of a smile as a natural response to feel-good emotions but did you know that smiling – even if that smile is faked – boosts your mood and reduces stress? Research done by psychology and facial-coding expert Paul Ekman and backed up by recent research published in *Psychological Science* found that a big smile that involves facial-muscle activity around the eyes produces a change in brain activity and mood.[1]

This research points to one simple but wonderful conclusion: smiling will make you feel better. (Frowns actually have the opposite effect.) If you don't feel like smiling that doesn't matter because, as I'll explain later, faking a smile that involves eye and mouth muscles will still work, especially so if you do it to yourself in the mirror, as there is great power in looking at your own reflection. So

Ritual #5 asks you to look in the mirror every morning and give yourself the gift of a great big smile.


## THE BENEFITS

> 'We shall never know all the good that a simple smile can do.'
> Mother Teresa

Smiling boosts your mood and generates positive emotions because it actually changes your brain. Children smile a lot more than adults (around 300 times a day compared to our 20 or so smiles) and that is probably why children make us feel happier.[2] Studies also suggest that smiling can reduce stress and be as energizing as a good night's sleep.[3] There is even a study carried out by Wayne State University, based on a yearbook, which indicated that those who had the biggest smiles lived longer and happier lives.[4]

All the above mood- and life-enhancing benefits are not just about you because if you smile more during your day you also lift the moods of others. UCLA scientist Marco Iacoboni has noted that if one person sees another smiling, neurons in that person's brain that are wired for sociability light up as if they were actually smiling themselves.[5] So smile at yourself a lot in the mirror but don't forget to share some of those life-enhancing benefits with your loved ones and by smiling more in public during the day too.

There is also significant power in this ritual because it involves mirror work. Self-help icon Louise Hay pioneered the technique of mirror work in her bestselling book *You Can Heal Your Life* to encourage people to meet the most important person in their lives – themselves – and to remind them that their relationship with themselves influences everyone and everything in their lives (see also the discussion about self-esteem on page 21). In short, the more you love and accept and believe in yourself the more others will reflect that back to you. So the place to start building your self-confidence is by looking at the man or the woman in the mirror.


## ANECDOTAL EVIDENCE

'Mirror, mirror on the wall.'

*Snow White and the Seven Dwarfs*

Smiling has often seemed like second nature to me but when I started to give talks and release videos about my writing, my nerves and concern about how I would be perceived (I wanted to be taken seriously) meant I lost my smile. If you go on my Facebook video library you will see how my very first nervous videos received a muted reaction from readers.

Then as my confidence grew I naturally began to smile more and the more I smiled the more views I got. I practised my talks in front of the mirror and saw for myself that it was entirely possible to talk about even serious subjects with a positive expression on my face, and that it was impossible not to smile too much.

When I started to invite other writers and experts on my page to do short videos, I noticed the same thing. The videos just felt warmer and got more views when the person smiled more. I even found myself giving out advice to those who wanted to post, telling them to re-film and smile more. I heard myself saying, 'Just smile more. Practise in front of the mirror.' Many would reply saying that it didn't feel natural to smile when they didn't feel like it or it didn't feel appropriate. I told them to fake it and the reason I told them that is that I had done some research on smiling which had turned my thinking upside down because I discovered that faking a smile actually has the same beneficial effects on ourselves and others.[6]

When we feel good we smile, but – and this is crucial – when we smile this tells our brain to feel good. Once the muscles in your face smile neuro signals travel to your brain to trigger positive emotions. In this way smiling has the same mood-boosting effects on our brain as exercise. Indeed some research has gone onto suggest that it can feel as good as winning the lottery or eating a bar of chocolate![7]

I also learned that when we practise smiling in front of the mirror we can learn to smile bigger and wider, and this in itself can make us feel better.

## ROADBLOCKS

'Every time you smile at someone, it is an action of love, a gift to that person, a beautiful thing.'

Mother Teresa

Practising smiling in the mirror can feel a little embarrassing at first but if that is your roadblock read about the benefits of smiling more and how research confirms how powerful practising smiling can be. Don't let embarrassment, especially when nobody is looking, block your progress.

If you think you are a bit like Victoria Beckham and you don't think a smile flatters you there are ways to work around that. If you look at Mrs Beckham's photos she may not be smiling but there is a still a smile there in her facial muscles. There is a hint of a smile and her eyes (if they are not hidden by sunglasses) are laughing. Of course, a great big smile is more beneficial but if this is a step too far for you take inspiration from the Mona Lisa. There is a reason why this painted has captured the imagination for centuries. It is all about that enigmatic hint or glimpse of a smile.

If you are someone who doesn't find smiling comes natural you may be concerned that people will notice the difference between a real and a fake smile if you showcase your newly learned smile to others. The Duchenne smile (named after the scientist who first separated the mouth-corners smile from the eye-socket smile) is the true smile and our brains can distinguish between what is real and what is fake, but if we practise our smiles it truly is almost impossible for others to determine if it is fake. More about learning how to smile below.

Don't be concerned that people will perceive you as a weak person if you smile more. The opposite is true. The more comfortable you become with smiling the more comfortable people feel around you. Just change your thinking about smiling.

Finally, if you are worried people won't take you seriously if you smile then you need to watch a few videos of famous people or leaders. Notice how effectively they use their smiles and how it empowers rather than diminishes their message or advice. As mentioned above our brains are wired for imitation, so if you are worried about being the only person smiling, don't be. Keep smiling and in time others will smile along with you. If they don't then you need to think about why you are spending time with people who are so resistant to joy.

# PRACTICE: HOW TO SMILE

Every morning as you get dressed and ready for the day take a moment to look in the mirror and practise your smile.

Look yourself in the eyes, stand tall and meet yourself with the biggest of smiles.

Practise so that your smile involves both the corners of your mouth and your eye sockets. Remember that the brain picks up on facial-muscle movement and even if you don't feel great it will invoke positive emotions in some way. Then during the day bring your new smile out as often as you can. Even do it when you work or talk on the phone. People sense when someone is smiling when they talk to you and can't see you.

## BRINGING THE RITUAL TO LIFE

'If you smile when no one else is around, you really mean it.'
Andy Rooney

The simple act of practising smiling in front of the mirror becomes ritualized when you combine that with visualization that has deep meaning for you. So before you do your morning smile, remember a time in your life when you were really happy, in love or feeling very satisfied and fulfilled. Not only will this ritualize what you are doing by filling it with deep meaning it will also increase the likelihood of your smile being real and genuine.

# FOR THE RECORD

**Life-changing ritual:** Practise your smile in the mirror each morning.

**The theory:** This will boost your mood and the happier you look and feel, the greater your chances of attracting success and good feeling from others.

**The practice:** Notice how differently your day goes when you smile. How do others respond to you when you smile? What can a smile bring you in return? We tend to mirror what we see in the world, so if others see you are smiling and looking positive, they are likely to smile and be positive to you in return. See if the attitude of others changes toward you and, more importantly, if you feel better about yourself through the 21 days.

## DO IT: SMILE IN THE MIRROR!

So, if you want to look good and help yourself and others live longer, healthier and happier lives you know the answer – SMILE.

Start your day by practising in the mirror with an enormous smile and carry that smile around with you during the day. Smiling is a simple but too often neglected superpower that can significantly improve your life and the lives of others.

From now on, let your mirror and your smile be your best friends.

'Sometimes your joy is the source of your smile, but sometimes your smile is the source of your joy.'

Thich Nhat Hanh

# LIFE-CHANGING RITUAL #6

# SEE THE FINISH LINE

'Thoughts become things.'

Mike Dooley

One of the simplest but most exciting things we should all be doing first thing in the morning, because it boosts our chances of success and happiness greatly during the day, is to take a few moments to visualize all the good things that the future holds for us. Visualizations really can come true if we take the necessary steps in our lives to encourage their reality to manifest.

There is tremendous power in visualizing. Simply picture yourself having a super-productive day and achieving your goals. This is a technique athletes and sportspeople have used with great success. They see themselves reaching the finishing line or winning a game.[1] It is a technique that works for many of them and it can work for you. In your mind you can prepare for your best day ever by picturing it.

## THE BENEFITS

'I never hit a shot, not even in practise, without having a very sharp in focus picture of it in my head.'

Jack Nicklaus

Some studies have suggested that mental preparation is nearly as effective as physical practice but doing both together is by far the most effective.[2-4] Many sports and business people, inventors, artists, chess players, computer programmers, musicians and performers use vivid imagery that engages their senses to mentally rehearse what they hope to achieve or succeed or win. The late and great Muhammed Ali famously used visualization to ensure he remained 'the greatest'.

So if sports people and performers and inventors have successfully used the technique of visualization, there is no reason why anyone can't use it to enhance their chances of success in all areas of their lives. Studies have repeatedly shown that the mind–body connection is a powerful one[5] and that thoughts can influence behaviour, so armed with that knowledge we should all be taking care of our thoughts and making sure we use them to maximize our chances of success.

## ANECDOTAL EVIDENCE

'Visualize this thing you want. See it. Feel it. Believe in it. Create your mental blue print and begin.'

Robert Collier

Matthew Nagle is a quadriplegic. He was stabbed violently several years ago and is now paralysed from the neck down.

He blows into a tube to power the motor of his wheelchair and his arms and hands are strapped to the armrest. Despite this, Nagle can play computer games, open emails, operate a TV and control a robotic arm with his thoughts alone. He has transformed his life with mental training and in his case this training took just four days. There is a silicon chip implanted in his brain that can interpret his thoughts.

Matthew's story is an exceptional one so let's get back to the more everyday. I could give countless examples of how the power of visualization has transformed my life but would like to step aside and give the spotlight here to one of my readers, called Emma, who sent me her story.

'Theresa, I've had a really complex and difficult relationship with my daughter for years. We simply did not get on and there was a lot of hostility on both sides. I don't want to go into the details as too personal but after my husband died the distance between us got so bad that she didn't even invite me to her wedding. That hurt me deeply especially as the wedding day was on the same day as the second anniversary of my husband, my daughter's father's, passing. I believe she deliberately chose that date because she wanted him there in spirit but for me it was doubly cruel as I sat there alone, with my husband in heaven and my daughter getting married without her mother there.

'I tried everything Theresa. I wrote her letters and tried to explain and ask for reconciliation. I apologized even though I felt I had nothing to apologize for. Nothing... and then I read a feature online about how visualization could heal relationships. I was at a very low point in my life and willing to try anything so I decided to give it a try.

'Every morning and evening for five weeks I picture my daughter and me having a conversation and ending that conversation with a hug. I imagined every detail. At first it felt really awkward and when I tried to hug her in my imagination it was like trying to hug a stone and my mind found it hard to mentally embrace her but I stuck with it because even after the first time I visualized this scene when I finished I felt slightly better. So much so that I looked forward to trying again to see if it would be easier. You know, Theresa, it did get easier and after about two weeks started to get easier and easier. Four weeks in I was having the most warm and wonderful conversations with my daughter in my mind. It made me feel better. I thought it was the best I could hope for. I gave up trying to contact her and resigned myself.

'Then a miracle happened. I was rushing to get to work one morning and my mobile rang. It was my daughter. I picked it up and could hear she was crying. I told her I loved her and she told me she did too. She was calling to say she was pregnant and I was going to be a grandmother.

'In the weeks that followed my daughter and I spent a lot of time together getting to know each other and trying to understand the huge rift that had occurred. She showed me the video of her wedding so I could be there in spirit just as my husband was. I'm writing to you because a week ago she gave birth to her first child, a beautiful baby girl called Tracey – and this is the real miracle – the second name they gave her was Emma, my name.'

Another much-cited study published in the *Research Quarterly of the American Association for Health*[6] in the 1960s compared the effect of mental practice with that of physical practice in the development of a motor skill, the Pacific Coast 1 hand foul shot. In this study 144 high school boys were split into physical and mental practice groups on the basis of arm strength, intelligence and experience. Mental practice was found to be nearly as effective as physical practice under the conditions of the experiment. Later, in 1994, a meta-analysis of 35 studies found that mental practice, although not as good as physical practise, still enhanced performance.[7]

There is so much powerful anecdotal evidence for the power of visualization that Ritual #6 could dominate this whole book and if you haven't read *The Secret* by Rhona Byrne you may want to read that now as you will find so many compelling testimonials to the power of positive visualization to transform lives.

## ROADBLOCKS

'I would visualize things coming to me. It would just make me feel better. Visualization works if you work hard. That's the thing. You can't just visualize and go eat a sandwich.'

Jim Carrey

Visualization sounds like the easiest technique in the world. Simply daydream or create images in your mind but when you actually try, it isn't always that easy. Some of us have a very visual mind but others, and I'm one of them, sometimes find it hard or impossible. I think I am more of an auditory and kinaesthetic person than visual and this may be the case for you. You may find it hard to see the details or pictures in your mind's eye.

If you find visualization or seeing pictures in your mind on command impossible the problem here is not you but the limitations of the English language to visualize. There are a lot of other senses that you can use to visualize other than vision or seeing in pictures. Seeing in your mind's eye doesn't just mean seeing in pictures, it also includes envisioning with your mind's touch, smell, sound and taste. In other words, you can visualize something with your other inner senses. In India the meaning of the word envision or visualize used by Yogis makes all this clear. However, our language doesn't have words for those kinds of experiences so we are left with a word that is restricted and misleading because vision may be one of the least important senses to use when you visualize.

Vision is very left-brained. It keeps things at a distance but sound, smell and taste make things feel real. So if inner vision isn't your strongest sense visualize with your other senses.

Another roadblock is not getting immediate success. You enjoy a glorious visualization but don't see results. If that's the case you need to do your visualizations with real purpose and desire. You need to stay hopeful and excited and fan the fire within you. More importantly, you also need to preserve. You cannot expect to achieve success and create changes overnight. Sure, immediate success can happen but it usually takes time and the most important ingredient to add to your visualization is to act and take initiative in your daily life – not just visualize and wait passively for things to happen. Visualization can light the match in your mind, heart and spirit, but to create a fire there needs to be effort in the real world on your part.

Remember, this book is all about providing the missing part of the puzzle when it comes to the positive-thinking movement. No amount of positive thinking or visualization will work if you don't take action.

# PRACTICE: HOW TO DREAM BIG

As we get older we don't tend to dream and imagine as much as we did when we were children so this technique requires you to connect with your inner child again. When you get up in the morning spend a few moments visualizing the day ahead going brilliantly. See it as if it were a picture you have taken on your mobile. See it in your mind's eye as if it is happening right now and you are living in the picture. See things going well and people fully engaged with you and drawn to you. See opportunities coming your way. See yourself working hard and productively and handling everything that the day brings your way. See yourself resisting the urge to procrastinate. I'm putting the emphasis on the process here rather than the outcome because visualizing yourself taking the actions you need to take to help you succeed is far more effective than visualizing the actual outcome.

As you create this picture in your head, try to engage your senses. What do you see? What do you hear? What do you smell? What do you taste? See every detail down to what you are wearing. If anything hesitant or negative enters your picture delete it. This is your vision. You control what is or is not there. Only allow in what you want to see there. And above all when you visualize keep your desire and your positive expectation levels high. You need to picture what you want with real desire and interest.

You may want to do this immediately after you have completed Ritual #3 and asked yourself the Steve Jobs question see page 25) or you may want to do it as you get dressed and have breakfast. The important thing is that you do it. It only takes a few moments. The first time you do try this it may take a little getting used to, and you may need to find somewhere peaceful to sit and dream, but I hope that by the time you have reached 21 days it will feel completely natural and you will enjoy your morning movies in your head as you go about your usual morning routine.

## BRINGING THE RITUAL TO LIFE

'The mind is everything. What you think you become.'

Buddha

You can transform anything you do or think or say into a ritual by filling it with deep meaning. In the case of visualization simply remind yourself that thoughts and images are magical things. They have great power 'and with it comes great responsibility', to quote from the Spiderman movies. Be aware that what you picture in your mind and what you pay attention to with your thoughts and feelings can often manifest into reality. Armed with this knowledge be extremely careful what you wish for – because it might just happen.

## FOR THE RECORD

**Life-changing ritual:** Spend a few moments each morning visualizing a successful day.

**The theory:** This will create a picture for your mind that your daily life can mirror. Neurons in your brain interpret imagery as equivalent to real-life action.

**The practice:** Once you've become accustomed to this practice, aim to increase the power of your visualizations by making them bigger, brighter and louder, as this makes them more real to your mind. Turn up the volume on what you hear, make the sights brighter, and the emotions warmer and more positive. At the end of each day, write down any observations, whether it's that you're feeling more positive or that more opportunities are coming your way for bringing your visualization into reality.

### DO IT: SEE THE FINISH LINE!
Do you recall the scene in *The Matrix* when Neo opens his eyes and says, 'I know Kung Fu.'

Wouldn't we all like to learn things that fast and Ritual #6 has shown you that, although it may not happen as fast as it did for Neo, you can use the power of your mind to achieve success using the tried-and-tested technique of visualization. Supercharge that power by ritualizing it and using it alongside actual practice and taking action in your daily life and in time your dreams really will come true.

'To achieve great things we must first dream, then visualize, then plan, believe and act.'

Alfred A. Montapert

# LIFE-CHANGING RITUAL #**7**

# TUNE IN

'Do you know that your soul is composed of harmony?'
Leonardo da Vinci

The right upbeat tune can make you feel on top of the world. We can't help but tap our feet, smile and feel better. Ritual #7 is great fun. It asks you to let that special tune be your soundtrack for the day. There is plenty of research to suggest that listening to a happy beat can help you pay attention and boost your emotional state considerably.[1]

## THE BENEFITS

'If I were not a physicist, I would probably be a musician. I often think in music. I live my daydreams in music. I see my life in terms of music.'
Albert Einstein

There was a time once when listening to music through your headphones was considered by some to be detrimental to clear thinking but research has now proved this old-fashioned approach was utterly wrong. As long as the music isn't played too loud so it damages your hearing research has shown that listening to and studying and creating music can be extremely beneficial to brain function.[2]

We now know that the thought patterns that arise when listening to or making music can boost learning and social skills. It seems that the human brain works in a similar way to musical patterns. Some studies have shown that musicians have better interaction between the right and left sides of the brain, while others suggest that listening to music can transmit signals that activate other parts of the brain.[3] The 'Mozart effect' is a term most often used to describe the brain-boosting power of music, in that a study demonstrated that listening to classical music – in particular a Mozart piano sonata – increased IQ. The study was repeated on rats and they also showed increased skill in navigating mazes when exposed to the same music. Other studies have shown that music not only has stress-relieving and therapeutic properties but can also elevate mood. In other words, the right music can make you feel good.[4]

It isn't entirely clear how music boosts brainpower and mood but one thing is clear – it plays a beneficial role in cognitive function, lifting our spirits, and increasing stress relief and social skills. Music is the universal language of the heart and has a positive effect not just on brain function but also on so many areas of our lives. Making it a part of our morning routine is a sure-fire way to get your day off to the best possible start.

## THE ANECDOTAL EVIDENCE

'Today like every other day we wake up empty and frightened. Don't open the door to study and begin reading. Take down a musical instrument.'

Rumi

Recently, I had the honour of interviewing for my blog the bestselling author of *Dying To Be Me*, Anita Moorjani, who had a compelling near-death experience that completely changed her attitude to life. When I spoke to her I could sense the joy and energy coming from this lovely woman and I asked her for some tips to pass onto my readers. She had a few but said one of her secrets was every morning she put on her favourite song, 'Dancing Queen' by Abba, and however stressed or tired she felt, it boosted her mood and made her day before it had even started.

I could immediately identify with what she said because music has always had a special place in my heart. In my teenage years I had aspirations to become a ballet dancer and trained to a very high level but looking back I can see that it was more about the heavenly music of Tchaikovsky's *Nutcracker* and *Swan Lake* that enchanted me. If the music didn't speak to my heart I lost my desire to dance. It was the same a decade or so later when I became a health and fitness instructor for many years. I loved inspiring people to get fit but deep down it was the music. I spent hours mixing my tapes for my classes, combining both modern and classical music in a way that would bring maximum inspiration and within a year or so my classes were so packed the health clubs simply couldn't cope.

Anyone that did my classes at the time in central London in the Holmes Place health clubs will remember the music and incredible energy created. The atmosphere truly was electric. Of course, I worked people extremely hard in the classes (I used the tough discipline of my professional ballet training to ensure the classes were challenging) and I hope people's aerobic fitness benefited as a result but for me it was still all about the music. The reason I was able to get people to work so hard was because I deliberately chose music that just gave you a buzz and a zest for life.

Then for copyright reasons changes were made regarding the use of music in classes in health clubs and all instructors were told to use standard and approved music tapes or face a fine. I immediately stopped teaching fitness as a result. One of the greatest compliments people gave me when I taught fitness classes was that they always left feeling happy. I knew that was partly because of the movement and benefit to their fitness levels but even more so because of listening to great music.

## ROADBLOCKS

'Music expresses that which cannot be put into words and that which cannot remain silent.'

Victor Hugo

As we get older we often tend to listen to music less and less. I know my teenager children are barely without their head-phones but it does not come so natural to me and as we get older music doesn't feature so strongly in our lives anymore. Another regrettable thing about getting older is that we forget the importance of fun as life gives us so many responsibilities, but for this ritual I'm going to ask you to think young and let fun in. Just ditch conventional ideas about what is appropriate or not for a person your age, choose your favourite upbeat (and dare I say it, fun) song and put your headphones on for a few moments every morning. If after 21 days you don't think it has made a difference you can go back to a life without music.

If your roadblock is due to not owning any headphones or music, that is easily sorted. Headphones are not expensive and can be easily purchased anywhere and you can download your favourite songs from the Internet onto your phone. Can't think of a song? Not a problem. Here is a list of 10 songs that will instantly put a smile on your face.

- 'Dancing Queen' or 'Mamma Mia' by Abba
- 'Wake Me Up Before You Go Go' by Wham
- 'Walking on Sunshine' by Katrina and the Waves
- 'Beautiful Day' by U2
- 'The Bare Necessities' from the *Jungle Book*
- 'Don't Stop Believing' by Journey
- 'Come on Eileen' by Dexys Midnight Runners
- 'Don't Stop Me Now' by Queen
- 'Hey Ya' by Outkast
- 'Good Vibrations' by the Beach Boys

Of course, these tracks are by no means written in stone and best thing is you choose what sings to you, just make sure it is upbeat and makes you feel like dancing. And if you prefer classical music by all means choose that as long as the piece is relatively upbeat. Indeed, a recent study from the University of Helsinki has shown that classical music has a tempo-regulating effect on genes that are responsible for generating feelings of pleasure but also points out that it is highly likely any type of music can also have this positive effect.[5]

Finally, if you don't think you can find the time or the opportunity to listen to your song there are plenty of opportunities. You only need to listen to a few minutes to get the full effect. Put your headphones on as you prepare your breakfast or get dressed or do your exercise or brush your teeth. I never forget to brush my teeth and I have trained myself to put my headphones on and listen to my favourite upbeat song, 'Hey Ya', while brushing. I used to have regular fillings but not since I introduced this ritual into my life: I enjoy the song so much I put a lot of energy into brushing my teeth really well.

# PRACTICE: HOW TO USE YOUR MORNING SONG

This ritual couldn't be simpler or more fun. At some point in your morning routine be sure to put your headphones on and listen to at least two minutes of your favourite energizing song. The music should not be played too loud or too soft, just at a comfortable level, and if you feel like singing along go ahead as singing also has reported therapeutic effects for mind, body and soul.

## BRINGING THE RITUAL TO LIFE

'The highest goal of music is to connect one's soul to their divine nature.'

Pythagoras

As you listen to your song don't think about anything but the music. Feel the energy and feel the joy. Dance if you want to. Make this a sacred moment of happiness that is going to inspire the rest of your day.

## FOR THE RECORD

**Life-changing ritual:** Listen to your favourite upbeat song every morning

**The theory:** This will energize your brain and boost your mood, and encourage you to let that happy feeling spill over into your day.

**The practice:** Consider bringing music into other parts of your day. For example, you might want to tune into a local music station and discover some new artists while doing the dishes or listen to an old favourite CD on your commute to work. When you get the opportunity, enjoy turning up the volume and dancing – you can wait until you're on your own if you're worried what others will think – to get you moving and feeling great. Observe how the music affects your mood.

### DO IT: TUNE IN!

Completing your morning rituals with a happy tune is the perfect way to prepare you for the day ahead. An upbeat song boosts your mood, wakes up your mind and energizes you in every way. The happier you feel at the start of your day the happier your day is likely to be. Best of all, happiness is infectious. You really have started to become the change you want to see in the world.

'Emotions of any kind can be evoked by melody and rhythm; therefore music has the power to form character.'

Aristotle

# MORNING CHECK POINT

Before you head off to start your day review the seven rituals below to make sure you have completed them all. For ease of reference you may want to photograph this list on your mobile or quickly jot them down on a piece of paper and fix to your mirror or fridge door.

**Ritual #1: Wake up earlier**

**Ritual #2: Stretch instead of reaching for your phone**

**Ritual #3: Ask yourself one simple question**

**Ritual #4: Just breathe**

**Ritual #5: Smile in the mirror**

**Ritual #6: See the finish line**

**Ritual #7: Tune in**

# PART II

# LIVE ON PURPOSE
# 7 LIFE-CHANGING DAYTIME RITUALS

'You can't just sit there and wait for people to give you that golden dream, you've got to get out there and make it happen for yourself.'

Diana Ross

The following seven rituals can be performed at any time during your working day or daily routine, in any order that works best for you. They are all designed to easily and naturally fit into your day and require very little time and indeed effort. Their aim is to get you focused on doing rather than thinking about doing.

It can be hard – as we all live increasingly busy lives – to incorporate mini-rituals into your daily routine but the astonishing benefits of stopping for a brief moment of sacredness and going above and beyond what you normally do will energize your day and remind you that you are giving yourself self-care, which is absolutely crucial for your self-esteem.

# LIFE-CHANGING RITUAL #**8**

# TIDY ONE THING

'The first step in crafting the life you want is to get rid of everything you don't want.'

Joshua Becker

You may not believe it but there truly is a direct relationship between decluttering and living the life of your dreams. If you are surrounded by chaos you tend to get stuck and any plans and dreams you have remain unrealized because you can't see clearly. Clutter may even stop you knowing what it is that you want out of life because the chaos of physical things is a symbol of confusion in other areas of our lives. You can't see the wood for the trees. It can be the plans and ideas you have that never get started or completed. It can be the things you postpone. It can be relationships that are confusing and unrewarding. It can be addictive behaviour or finances out of control and so on.

So Ritual #8 asks you to tidy just one thing each day above and beyond your usual domestic chores. That doesn't necessarily mean a dramatic and time-consuming spring clean of your house or office. It means ensuring that every single day at some point you find one thing to tidy or organize or discard, and that can be as simple and small as tidying your shoe cupboard or your coat pockets. It is not how much time you spend decluttering, it is the *act* of tidying itself that has the true power here to attract success into your life and you double that power when you ritualize it.

First, though, let's explore the benefits of decluttering in more detail.

## THE BENEFITS

'Clear your stuff. Clear your mind.'

Eric M. Riddle

Tidying – even if it is just one thing – cleans up our lives physically, mentally, emotionally and spiritually. It liberates us from feeling trapped or stuck and becomes a catalyst for positive action. Research actually shows that the stress hormone cortisol is released when we are surrounded by disorder[1] so the first thing to benefit from a tidy up is your health because it is well documented that stress is bad news for our wellbeing.

The next thing to benefit is your concentration and creativity. Too much clutter in your environment can negatively impact how you focus according to neuroscientists at Princeton University. The study investigated how people performed in various tasks when they were in an organized and then a disorganized environment. Their study conclusively showed that clutter distracts attention and the result is a decrease in performance and focus.[2] Clutter essentially makes your brain multitask rather than focus on the task in hand. So releasing that clutter can boost your creativity and focus.

According to an article by Christopher Peterson, PhD in *Psychology Today*, clutter can affect us psychologically and he references a study published in the *Journal of Applied Developmental Psychology* to back that up. This study looked at the effects of a chaotic, noisy, disorganized and cluttered environment on children. It showed that there clearly is a link between clutter and lack of concentration and creativity.[3]

If you are feeling overwhelmed or confused just taking a few moments to tidy your desk or workplace can have immediate results. Much, of course, depends on the type of person you are, what you need to focus on and the levels of concentration required but in the majority of cases a minimalist environment can boost the creative process.

Another unknown benefit of tidying up is that it might help you relax and sleep better. A sleep study has shown that people who sleep in untidy rooms are more likely to have sleeping disorders.[4] In addition, clutter can make you feel irritable because it sends your brain a signal that your life is disorganized. Researchers from the UCLA Center on Everyday Lives of Families proved this link as they studied 32 families and found that those who had the greatest amount of 'stuff', and disorganization as a result, had the highest stress levels.[5]

Then there is the emotional baggage we associate with things. Sometimes we keep things from our past around us that actually drag us down because they have negative associations. Decluttering can give us a chance to clean up our lives emotionally and make a fresh and bright new start. We hoard many more items than we need and instead of adding to our lives they become things that slow us down so the message here is to get rid of things that drag you down, or make you feel guilty, like that exercise bike you never use or the juicer you keep meaning to use but never do.

Letting go of the clutter is like letting go of your past and that's not always easy but if you tidy one thing, however small, you will find that the benefits outweigh any negatives.

## ANECDOTAL EVIDENCE

'When we clear the physical clutter from our lives, we literally make way for inspiration and "good, orderly direction" to enter.'

Julia Cameron

In my personal experience I have seen dramatic results from regular decluttering, as it is a way to fast-forward change. Nature doesn't tolerate a vacuum so releasing clutter invites something else into its place. Time and time again when I feel overwhelmed or uncertain about the best way forward, I have found that decluttering my work or living space brings clarity and a burst of direction, focus and energy.

There are so many anecdotal reports of the benefits of decluttering to choose from among my friends but I will talk about a journalist I worked with many years ago. She had the most brilliant mind. I really enjoyed working with her, as it was impossible not to feel inspired by her creativity. The problem was that her brilliant plans never ever materialized. They were constantly stuck in the idea phase. At first it was quite endearing but after a while it got very frustrating because I'm one of those people who like to see results, so I ended up doing both her work and my own. We got to the end of the job and then a few months down the line we were asked to team up again. This time I had some reservations so we arranged to meet up at her flat and talk through working together again.

When I stepped through her front door I could see the absolute chaos she was living in. I could not believe it. Stacks of books and magazines – some of them open – lying on the floor. Bottles, bags, gloves, everything under the sun on the floor and the kitchen had dishes piled up in the sink. I could go on. The chaos was out of this world and comparable now to what I see when I walk into my 17-year-old son's bedroom. I asked her how she could live in this way and she had no answer. I told her about my dilemma with working with her again and that this time I wasn't going to do her work. She agreed and then asked if I could help her get organized because she really didn't know how. My instinct immediately told me that the place to start was with her home.

Right there and then I offered to help her tidy up and for the next three days I went round to her flat after work. We could have filled a skip with the amount of junk we threw away.

At the end her flat was beautiful and spacious and it was like a weight had lifted from her shoulders. She looked years younger and happier. With her home decluttered, we did the same for her desk at work and she made a promise to me to keep control of the junk she let into her life. The decluttering worked because there was a new focus about her. She was no longer distracted and when it came to delivering our subsequent projects together she actually sent her work in before me and if I'm totally honest it was better than mine.

I've lost touch with her now but know she won't mind me using her as anecdotal evidence here to illustrate the benefits of decluttering. She told everyone at the time how much my advice had helped her find her focus. I truly hope she kept that focus because she was a brilliant journalist.

## ROADBLOCKS

'The more I examine the issue of clutter, the more effort I put into combating it, because it really does act as a weight.'

Gretchen Rubin

The most common roadblock to decluttering is lack of time but it is important to understand that decluttering is never a waste of time and can in the long run give you more time. For example, if you spend precious time every morning trying to find your spectacles or phone or keys but can't because there is so much clutter hiding them, then that is time wasted every day. However, if you tidy up so you can easily find your essential items then you save that time each day. If you need to find information quickly in work or life a disordered environment will hinder that so tidying up your environment will make you more productive in the long run.

Another reason people give for not decluttering is that they get attached to things and want reminders of their past around them but this is still no reason for chaos. You can keep items that have meaning but why the stuff that drags you down? Also things are just that – 'things'. It is the memories in your heart and mind that matter. A family friend of mine lost many personal items several years ago when her home and workplace was burgled. At first she was hugely upset as there were financial implications and the items meant a great deal to her but eventually it made her realize how much more important it was that her children weren't in when it happened and that nobody had got hurt. She realized that the thieves had just taken 'stuff', and 'stuff' is not essential for our happiness.

If you are one of those people who say they operate best in chaos that may well be the case because the emphasis here is on how your environment makes you feel. Everybody has a difference tolerance for disorder and some people function better when there is some mess in their surroundings. It is often the case that a highly creative person's desk will look pretty chaotic and photos of Steve Jobs' workspace prove that point. Less is not always more. The important thing here is your perception of clutter. If you feel perfectly comfortable in your home and workspace, and it does not distract your attention then it won't negatively impact you. However, if you constantly feel overwhelmed and can't find things or have no idea where things are, it is time for a sort out. The key word here is ease. You need to live and work in an environment where you feel at ease.

Having said that, even the messiest of people can still benefit from a little order in their chaos and the benefits of decluttering for their health in mind, body and spirit remain the same. If too many things are surrounding you and competing for your attention then it will be harder to focus. And if you are one of those people who are naturally tidy and would have trouble knowing what to tidy up for this ritual then there is always something that can be done with a sense of sacredness: for example, clearing your desktop or improving your calendar or diary system or organising old messages and email into folders and so on.

Finally, the biggest excuse for not decluttering is saying you simply can't face it. The task feels so overwhelming but if that is the case the important thing is to start small. Tidy one thing each day. Don't look at the bigger picture. Just start with one cupboard, one desk or part of your wardrobe or desktop and so on. Keep doing that and in good time you will find that harmony and order becomes a stronger theme in your life.

# PRACTICE:
# HOW TO DECLUTTER

Perform at least one act of decluttering a day and that act can be as big or as small as you like or take up as much or as little time as you like. It could be a big clean out of your wardrobe or simply tidying the receipts from your credit cards in your wallet or purse or sorting out the pens on your desk. It doesn't matter what you choose to tidy up – the important thing is that you make a conscious decision to declutter at least one thing a day. Remember, even the messiest and most highly creative of people could still benefit from incorporating Ritual #8 into their lives in any or all of the following subtle ways.

**Set limits:** Do bear in mind that clutter isn't just physical. It can also be digital. Anything that pings on your PC or phone or tablet, which isn't filed away or organized, creates a digital clutter that overloads your brain with too many to-dos. When our brain is overloaded it can't focus or multitask well or remember things. Every day of our lives new information comes flooding in so set a limit on how much you will take on board. There will always be more information than your brain can process so set limits so your brain does not get cluttered. Filter what you read. Don't reply to emails unnecessarily. Finish one book before you start another. Let your phone go to voicemail if the call isn't urgent or important to you. If you use a computer for work, having a desktop that is full of files can make you feel anxious so each day remove files that aren't essential or create a couple of folders on your desktop and drop relevant files in there so when you go to your computer you see a clean screen.

**One a day:** Try to get rid of rubbish or give to charity one item a day that you don't use or wear or need anymore. It could be as simple as a pen on your desk that has no refill to an item of clothing in your wardrobe that hangs there but you never wear. The crucial thing is that you tidy at least one thing in your life or work or online.

## BRINGING THE RITUAL TO LIFE

'When we throw out the physical clutter, we clear our minds. When we throw out the mental clutter, we clear our souls.'

Gail Blanke

Clutter in whatever form it takes – stuff or digital – is something that is a part of life but it can be controlled. Each day that you find a way to choose and control what information gets to you or stays with you will give you a sense of empowerment and clear your mind, leaving you the energy and space to eat the 'food' of your choice and not what others are force-feeding you.

Feng shui is the ancient Chinese practice of creating peaceful and harmonious surroundings that enhance the flow of life called *qi* (meaning energy, also known in other cultures as *chi* or *prana*). It is centuries old and is closely related to the wisdom of Tao. Its ultimate aim is to bring good fortune into all aspects of your life and clutter is most certainly something that will work against that aim. I've recommended a couple of books in the references section if you would like to explore feng shui further.

According to feng shui clutter represents stagnant energy and when there is clutter in your home or work there will be metaphorical clutter within you, mentally, emotionally, physically and spiritually. Consciously reminding yourself that when you are tidying up you are clearing out negative energy in all areas of your life makes it easy to transform the act of decluttering into a sacred ritual.

## FOR THE RECORD

**Life-changing ritual:** Tidy or declutter one thing.

**The theory:** This will increase your concentration and creativity and decrease stress.

**The practice:** Ensure that you stop and appreciate the benefits of living in a decluttered, tidy environment; notice how it changes how you feel about yourself. If you have a lot of decluttering to do, remember that every day you create a little more order is a step toward having more time, energy and creativity. If you're already quite organized, focus on being mindful as you tidy. Take a note of any correlation you observe between your levels of creativity and confidence and the act of decluttering.

## DO IT: TIDY ONE THING!

A clean and decluttered living space and workspace will maximize your productivity in all areas of your life. Science dictates that energy – in the form of heat or heat flow – is constantly flowing into and out of all objects, both living and dead, so every time you clear space you create dynamic energy shifts. Therefore letting go of old energies clears the space to create new ones. If you can declutter at least one thing in your life for the next 21 days you will feel lighter, happier, and more excited and focused as a result.

So make a start and notice what happens in your life. Watch for miracles.

> 'When you live surrounded by clutter, it is impossible to have clarity about what you are doing in your life.'
>
> Karen Kingston

# LIFE-CHANGING RITUAL #9

# FILL YOUR OWN CUP

'Enjoy life sip by sip not gulp by gulp.'

The Minister of Leaves

Ritual #9 encourages you to find a moment of peace when you make and/or drink a cup of tea, coffee or whatever drink you prefer. It draws inspiration from the sublime art of tea-drinking ceremonies practised for centuries in Asia.

You may wonder how something as simple as enjoying a cup of tea, or any drink of your choice, can change your life and it is connected not to the drink itself but to the state of mind this ritual encourages you to create. A beverage break is the perfect moment to give yourself a moment of peace and, more important than that, self-love. If you neglect your own needs success and happiness will elude you.

## THE BENEFITS

'Where there is tea there's hope.'

Sir Arthur Pinero

The chances are the drink you choose to take your time out with will be a cup of refreshing tea or an energizing coffee and research has shown that in both cases there are proven health benefits to enjoying a cup or two of these beverages a day.[1] Coffee and tea drinkers, for example, are said to be less likely to contract a number of diseases and cognitive decline is reduced.

For the purposes of this book, though, the most important benefit is that a tea or coffee break gives you some much-needed time to yourself to reflect. Common sense and scientific research agree that until you have met your own physical and emotional needs you can't muster sufficient resources for someone else. When you start to neglect yourself for the sake of others you simply can't be effective in helping them.

To live a happy and successful life you need a giving nature but first and foremost you need self-love. Successful people have learned how important self-care is to their wellbeing so they integrate it into their lives. Research has even shown that there are key differences between people who love themselves or esteem themselves highly and those who don't.[2] For example, people with high self-esteem focus on growth and improvement and moving forward, whereas those with low self-esteem are more prone to depression and fearful of making mistakes, so therefore are less likely to succeed.

There are many ways to build your self-esteem but ensuring you take some time out to enjoy a peaceful moment with your favourite drink each day is a great way to remind you of the vital importance of taking care of number one.

## ANECDOTAL EVIDENCE

'Coffee/tea is a hug in a mug.'

Unknown

There have been many times in my life when I have forgotten how important self-love is for happiness and success but one stands out and that is when I was in my mid-twenties and had my heart broken for the first time.

My whole life had been wrapped around my boyfriend. My identity merged into his and making him happy was all I cared about. He was my life and I thought this was going to last forever. For two years I lived my life around my boyfriend's every mood and whim – even when it was emotionally and physically abusive. When that happened I should have left but I wanted to help him, you see. I wanted to show him that I loved the bad and the good in him. I thought my love for him would transform him. I became attuned to his every need, constantly trying to prove my love to him. I wanted to be everything to him – to make myself indispensable.

This wasn't the first relationship that was defined by my eagerness to please, putting the needs of others before my own. More often than not my identity was defined by what others thought of me. If my friends were bored it was because I was boring. If my peers didn't have time for me it was because I didn't matter. If my boyfriend appreciated me I felt good about myself. If I couldn't match someone's need or mood I was terrified they would not like me – and not being liked was like a living death for me. I was making my life impossible because the harder I tried to win someone's respect, friendship or love the more I lost touch with who I was or what my needs were and the deeper my feelings of doubt became.

When my boyfriend left me for another woman I hit an all-time low but it was also a massive turning point in my life, for which I am forever grateful. The light-bulb moment of sudden clarity came one day after a conversation with a very wise woman who asked me why I was crying over someone who wasn't crying over me. Her words spoke so very clearly to me. Crying wasn't going to change anything. I couldn't change how my ex felt about me but I could change how I felt about myself. I did deserve better. Looking to a relationship to create good feelings about myself put all the power into the hands of someone other than myself. Why was I doing that?

I remember going home after my conversation with that woman and making myself a strong cup of tea. Her words empowered me so much. I sat down with that cup of tea in my hand and savoured the moment and the delicious taste, as I never had before. I sat there and had a good long think about my life. I realized that over the years I had been conditioned to believe that a good person is a selfless person but I needed to learn that being good is not the same as always putting the needs of others before your own.

Of course, we should all reach out to others in times of need and help ease their burdens if we can, but it is also important to honour and respect the spark of divinity that lives inside each one of us. I didn't need the approval of others or their acceptance. I wasn't being selfish if I disagreed or said no from time to time – I was paying attention to what boosted, rather than drained me. I was becoming a person of spirit. In short, seeking feelings of comfort and love from the inside out rather than the outside in.

Those quiet moments of reflection with a steaming brew in my hand truly changed my life and from then onwards, although my favourite beverage is now coffee instead of tea, I truly value times of quiet reflection with my favourite drink. It is my precious 'me' time and I value it highly. The day is not complete without it.

## ROADBLOCKS

'Better to be deprived of food for three days then tea for one.'

Chinese proverb

You may not be a tea or coffee drinker and that is perfectly fine as this ritual applies to any drink you have, even a glass of water. Remember it is not so much the drink itself but the act of taking a few moments in your day to reflect alone in peace about yourself and your life. It is about savouring the moment and giving yourself some time, space and peace. It is about filling your cup both metaphorically and literally so you have more to give others.

If your favourite drink is alcoholic that is perfectly fine as long as you restrict yourself to one glass a day, as any more than that and this ritual is no longer one of self-love because the toxic effects of excessive alcohol consumption on health, wellbeing and relationships are well documented. To a lesser degree too much caffeine from strong tea, coffee or sodas (such as cola or energy drinks) can also have a toxic effect so moderation in all things is always advised.

This ritual is ideally one that you perform alone but if friends or family or colleagues are always around and wanting to join you for your time out you could politely tell them that you just need some space or time to reflect. Perhaps you could organize for them to join you for another drink later in the day?

It is not selfish to take care of your needs or make your needs a priority from time to time or to ask others to give you space. You can't give to others what you don't have yourself. You have to love yourself enough to love others.

If you don't think you can afford the time out and tend to drink on the go the answer is simple: find the time. You only need to give yourself a few minutes of space and peace, and taking that time out will increase rather than decrease your productivity because this ritual is all about recharging your batteries. If a car runs out of fuel it stops running and it is the same with self-care. If you don't give yourself a little time and space each day to reflect and centre yourself you simply won't have a productive day.

If you find it hard to give to yourself in this way then you have identified a key factor in your life that will be blocking your chances of success and happiness. Ask yourself why giving to yourself is so hard. Happy and successful people have learned how important self-care is so they integrate it into their life.

Of course, urging you to love yourself more is easier said than done so here are a few tips that might help:

**Be your own best friend:** Treat yourself as you would treat your own best friend. Don't be harsh or unforgiving and speak to yourself gently and positively as you would to someone you loved.

**Avoid perfectionism:** Perfection is an impossible goal and will simply make you love yourself less. The only thing any of us can aspire to is being perfectly imperfect.

**Glass half full:** When you drink the beverage of your choice and get to the halfway point in your cup, remind yourself that it is half full and not half empty and then extend that idea to your daily life. Discard your negative filter and focus more on the positive than the negative – this is especially the case with thoughts that you have about yourself. Never call yourself names like 'failure' as that is defining yourself by one thing you did wrong, it is not defining all of you. This involves rewriting your inner script in a more positive way.

**Self-love is a choice:** Loving yourself is a choice you can make right now. You don't have to be thinner or more successful or pass that exam or get that job to love yourself – you can do it right here and right now. You can choose love at any time. It really is that simple. If you are not willing to love yourself today then you are not willing to love yourself tomorrow. Start today.

## PRACTICE: HOW TO DRINK YOUR DAILY CUP

At some point in your daily routine, take a few moments out to sit quietly by yourself with a drink of your choice and use this time to reflect and enjoy a moment of peace. It doesn't matter what drink you choose or when you do this – although mid-morning during the traditional coffee break is ideal – as what matters here is that this time is just for you. This is a time for you to think about how you feel and reflect on your life and your needs. This is your treat time.

## BRINGING THE RITUAL TO LIFE

'The Way of Tea is based on the simple act of boiling water, making tea, offering it to others and drinking it ourselves. Served with a respectful heart and received with gratitude, a bowl of tea satisfies both physical and spiritual thirst.'

Urasenke

Transforming a tea or coffee break into a ritual draws inspiration from the beautiful Japanese tea ceremony where tea drinking has deep spiritual significance. In Japan tea making is a meditation that enriches body, mind and soul.

Remind yourself as you take your time out to enjoy your favourite drink that this is about so much more than a few moments of peace. This is about you. This is about quietening your mind and listening to your heart and soul and loving you. Deep within our heart is the person who we really are – our core, our soul, our essence. Your soul knows your potential and your essence and whenever you aren't taking good care of yourself or looking in the wrong place for happiness and success your soul will let you know.

Listen to your soul: all your questions have an answer if you can learn to hear it. Discover what you need and what truly drives you from within and then match it with real-world activities to give your life purpose and meaning.

## FOR THE RECORD

**Life-changing ritual:** Take some quiet time out for yourself each day to enjoy your favourite beverage.

**The theory:** This will encourage you to focus on your own needs and the crucial importance of self-love.

**The practice:** Take care not to spend this precious time on your phone or worrying about your to-do list. Instead focus on mindful drinking and if you find yourself getting lost in thoughts, simply bring your focus back to the cup in your hand and the sensations of drinking. Be sure to choose a beautiful cup or mug too when you take your brew and spend a moment in gratitude for the tea (and the tea growers and the lorry drivers that brought it to your cup). Notice how this little self-care ritual brings you peace and joy, and see if there is a correlation between your feelings of happiness and taking time out to yourself.

## DO IT: FILL YOUR OWN CUP!

Never forget that your tea break is not about what you drink but about a state of mind, a way of changing your life by reminding you of the magic and love you can discover within yourself if you simply take some time out for yourself.

When you appreciate yourself and truly start to love yourself the whole world will start to respond. It is when you start to believe in magic again. So why not stop, put the kettle on and hitch your wagon to the stars?

'In the taste of a single cup of tea you will eventually discover the truth of all ten thousand forms of the universe.'

Zen master Kyongbongg Sunim, Ch'ann

# LIFE-CHANGING RITUAL #**10**

# LET IT GO

'Sooner or later we've all got to let go of the past.'

Dan Brown

Sorry isn't the hardest word for many of us – goodbye is. Many of us find it extremely hard to let go and we cling on to negative feelings that are preventing us from growing and moving forward with our lives, so Ritual #10 is all about releasing.

Letting go of negative emotions, or experiences or things or people who simply don't fit into your life anymore, is essential for changing your life for the better. Releasing is the key to personal growth but it doesn't come naturally to most of us. It is a practice and for the next 21 days I would like you to spend a little time releasing any feelings that are holding you back. We need to consciously decide to let go and repeatedly act in this way if we are to attract success and happiness into our lives.

## THE BENEFITS

'In the process of letting go you will lose many things from the past, but you will find yourself.'

Deepak Chopra

Research suggests that negative emotions, like fear, anger and guilt, release chemicals into your body that can weaken immunity and cause major illnesses, fatigue and poor health in general. Holding onto negative emotions can also seriously damage your psychological health and trigger depression.[1]

If you hold on to negative emotions they tend to dominate your perception of everything and everyone, and so sabotage your chances of success and happiness as a result. Releasing those emotions will also stop you worrying so much about what other people think because once you let go of what is dragging you down you rediscover your true self, and then the rest tends to sort itself out. In addition, releasing will encourage you to stop seeing yourself as a victim because when you see yourself in this way you are helpless to create the positive changes you need to transform your life. Accepting responsibility for your feelings, letting go and moving on is empowering because it puts you in control.

Letting go is not the same as ignoring or suppressing. In fact, it is quite the opposite. You must acknowledge negative feelings before letting go. Focusing exclusively on the positive while neglecting to give due attention to the negative emotions that have accumulated over the years is a recipe for disaster because in order to find a sense of meaning and personal growth in life you need to deal with both joy and pain. Bad feelings can also act as a warning sign alerting us to areas of our lives that aren't working so they must be acknowledged. So, while it is impossible to avoid negative feelings – after all, life is about experiencing setbacks and conflicts – the key is learning how to deal with them. Suppressing them or carrying them around with you will damage your health and psychological wellbeing. Acknowledging them, learning from them and then releasing them will increase your chances of health and happiness.

## ANECDOTAL EVIDENCE

'We must be willing to let go of the life we have planned, so as to have the life that is waiting for us.'

Joseph Campbell

When my mother died I couldn't let her go. I went into denial. I didn't want any of her personal items around me so I gave them all away and kept just a few personal items in a shoebox I stored under my bed. Whenever thoughts about her came into my head I buried myself in work. Facing the grief was too much to bear. I didn't cry. At her funeral I didn't feel fully present. It was as if I was watching myself and the service while not being a part of it. For several months after my mother died I didn't allow myself to cry.

If you are someone who has a healthy approach to grief and understands the importance of letting go, my denial may appear hard to understand but I am using it here as an extreme example of the dangers of not letting go and accepting that something important has left your life. Not surprisingly, this state of denial was too fragile to protect me from the reality of grief and six months after my mother died I plunged into full-blown depression, which took several years to pull out of. Looking back now I can see that I didn't need to hit the dark depths of despair and effectively waste two years of my life if I had been able to cry, grieve and let go of my mother in a healthy way.

Crucial to my recovery from depression was learning to let go of my mother, and the powerful ritual of releasing a sky lantern and watching it fly away at night played a major part in that process of letting go. I performed it every night for a month and slowly I was able to acknowledge my pain, release it, cry, grieve and move forward with my life. Along the way I also learned that the black hole of my depression wasn't just triggered by the denial of grief following the death of my mother but by other relationships, feelings and experiences in my past that I wasn't able to let go of. I was hoarding everything from my past like a magpie and it was weighing me down heavily.

Sometimes it was a case of simply recognizing that I was clinging on unnecessarily to something I had outgrown. For example, friends from various stages in my life that I had now grown apart from but still kept in touch with, even though it brought little sense of true connection. Other times it was a case of releasing something extremely toxic. For example, my anger and resentment at my father for being largely absent from my life, and the low self-esteem and lack of self-belief this generated in me; or my sorrow that I wasn't able to have the career of a ballet dancer, as I had dreamed of.

It was time to stop letting negative feelings and disappointments from my past define my present. I had to learn to acknowledge the pain, and let go to move on. I had to stop defining myself as a victim of my past and my feelings of hurt, grief and disappointment.

Today, letting go is something I do every day. It is something I believe I need to practise every day. It means accepting aspects of me that shaped the person I am today and living in the moment rather than through the filter of memories. It also means seeing myself as whole rather than broken or pulled in different directions. I practise a letting-go ritual every day because if I didn't I'm sure I would fall back into my old ways. Also, being a mother of two teenage children, letting go is so very important because I still tend to think of them as my babies, when I was their world, and I need to learn to accept them now as adults who love me but don't need me quite as much anymore. The way I let go is symbolic, through visual rituals – and I'll detail some of them below. This helps things feel really obvious and final to me but as with all these rituals the way you let go must be one that works for you. I can only offer suggestions here that have worked for me.

## ROADBLOCKS

'There is an important difference between giving up and letting go.'

Jessica Hatchigan

Most people are scared to admit they have inner pain because they think the process of letting go will open old wounds again and they will relive the pain. This isn't the case at all because you are not revisiting your inner pain, you are releasing it and letting it go. The process is completely natural and far less painful than the inner pain. Compare it to being shot by an arrow in the chest. The arrow could stay lodged in your chest and you may be able to survive but in time the wound will fester and turn poisonous and threaten your life. However, if the arrow is gently and painlessly removed you are free of it and ready to heal and live a normal and healthy life again.

Others may be scared of letting go of old wounds because they have become comfortable with using them as an excuse not to be happier or more successful. If that's the case the letting-go ritual in this chapter is absolutely crucial if you want to change your life for the better. A backward-looking victim mind-set is a barrier to success and happiness in every area of your life.

The choice is yours. You can choose to move in the direction of your dreams or you can choose to live a life of excuses where dreams do not come true.

Surprisingly, another roadblock for this ritual is not thinking you have anything to let go of. Perhaps you don't have painful memories from the past or feelings that drag you down. If that is the case letting go is still important because life is always about moving forward. You need to let go of stages in your life or people or situations that aren't quite a fit for you anymore. There is always something we need to let go of, whether we realize it or not, even if that letting go is simply saying goodbye with love and blessings to what happened yesterday.

## PRACTICE: HOW TO LET GO

As mentioned above it is important to find your own way to let go of emotions, situations, people or beliefs that no longer resonate with you or are holding you back.

Letting go is an on-going process for each one of us, even if we are not consciously aware of it, because if we think about it each day of our lives, to fully embrace the opportunities today presents we must let go of yesterday, so here are some suggestions to help that process. There isn't a separate section this time on how to ritualize this process because letting go is always deeply meaningful and therefore by definition a ritual.

First of all recall an emotional experience or situation that is causing you discomfort or sorrow or regret. Visualize it in your mind and then as you perform the ritual of your choice formally let go of that painful experience or feeling. If you don't have anything that you feel needs releasing simply focus on what went on in your life yesterday and releasing that to the past. Here are some suggestions:

**Gone with the wind:** This is one of my favourite letting-go rituals and one to be done outdoors. You simply pick up something light like a feather, blade of grass or a leaf and then blow on it and watch it float away. As it floats away I say goodbye to the past or to anything or anyone that I need to release. I love this ritual and can truly understand why many people find great comfort from releasing the ashes of a loved one into the wind.

**Ashes to ashes:** If you have time and the opportunity, writing down what you want to let go of on a piece of paper and then lighting a match and (safely) watching it burn can be a very powerful releasing ritual.

**Cut the cord:** If you have time and the opportunity take a balloon outside, cut the cord and watch it float away and as it does say goodbye to your past. Releasing a sky lantern when night falls can be as effective and perhaps even more beautiful. This is the beautiful and inspiring ritual that helped me cope following the loss of my mother.

**Float away:** Drop some flowers into a river and watch them float away. If you don't live near a river you can do this ritual whenever you release the plug in your sink.

**Create a space:** This can link in with Ritual #8 in that when you clear away clutter or tidy a space you can think of it also as a way of letting go of the old to make way for the new.

**Blessings:** If it is time to say goodbye to someone you have studied with, lived with, worked with or had an important relationship with, one of the most powerful ways to let go is to simply say goodbye with your blessing.

## BRINGING THE RITUAL TO LIFE

'May you be filled with loving kindness. May you be well. May you be peaceful and at ease. May you be happy.'

Ancient Tibetan Buddhist blessing

There are countless ways to let go but accompanying it with a visual or symbolic act can make the process easier to relate to. If you simply haven't got the time or the opportunity, a simpler way to complete this ritual is to breathe in deeply, hold the breath for a few seconds and then exhale slowly until you have no air left in your lungs. As you exhale say goodbye to your past or whatever you need to let go of.

After whatever ritual you choose to complete here be sure to give yourself a moment of celebration. Don't skip this important step because what you have done is a big deal. Emotions can trap you and drag you down and letting go like this can set you free. If on some days you feel like crying before performing this ritual let your tears become the ritual. Research shows that crying is a way of releasing and letting go of bacteria and toxins and there are great health benefits in crying.[2] Crying also relieves stress and improves mood and communication.

## FOR THE RECORD

**Life-changing ritual:** Spend a few moments each day releasing and letting go.

**The theory:** This will help you embrace the present moment more fully and prevent negative or unfulfilling emotions, relationships and situations from holding you back.

**The practice:** Enjoy the sense of lightness you feel, as you let go of anything that's been holding you back. Note down whether there is a correlation between your letting-go ritual and your ability to seize the moment and see a clear way ahead as you progress through the 21 days.

## DO IT: LET IT GO!

Nobody wants to experience emotional pain but it is a part of life and if we hold onto that hurt we accumulate emotional baggage that stops us moving on. According to Buddha we are given 10,000 joys and 10,000 sorrows and our challenge is to not get overwhelmed by either the joy or the pain but to keep our hearts open and loving instead of closed and cold.

Performing a letting-go ritual consistently for the next 21 days can help release negative energy from your past so you are free to welcome new and exciting experiences and endless love and happiness into your heart and your life. You are clearly drawing a line between yesterday and today. You are letting go and moving on to something new and better and that is what a meaningful, exciting and happy life is all about.

'Life moves forward. The old leaves wither, die and fall away and the new growth extends forward toward the light.'
Bryant McGill

# LIFE-CHANGING RITUAL #11

# SAY A LITTLE PRAYER

'Seven days without prayer makes one weak.'

Allen E. Vartlett

All the rituals in this book are designed to help you manifest what you want in life but this one is the spiritual powerhouse. That's why it is firmly placed centre stage. It's based on the very simple concept of knowing what you want and believing you can have it. It's all about the life-changing power of prayer or intention.

It's about directing your thoughts entirely towards what you want to happen or manifest in your life. The more you believe and invest energy in those thoughts the more likely they are to happen. Don't get distracted by the details or the obstacles or any doubts or fears that stand in your way, just keep focused on your dreams. You need to train your mind to totally believe that what you really, really want will one day happen.

You may be thinking at this point that I'm simply returning to the power of the positive-thinking mantra of many a self-help book, but that isn't the case at all. This book is about doing rather than thinking about doing and as you read on you will see that this life-changing ritual is absolutely no exception.

## THE BENEFITS

'If you only pray when you are in trouble... you're in trouble.'
Anonymous

The idea of optimism leading to better health has been studied and the message that comes across loud and clear is that a positive attitude definitely improves both physical and mental health. Science has also shown that there truly is healing power in prayer, although these studies are mainly focused on the health benefits of prayer for people with strong religious leanings.[1] Other research on positive thinking and intention, however, clearly shows that focused thinking has great power.[2] It's impossible to know how this works exactly but it may have something to do with the law of return or what you give out you get back. You could compare it to throwing a ball into the air. You know it is going to fall back to the ground at some point. In other words, what you think or focus on with great passion will manifest in your life in some way.

Perhaps you have noticed this in your life or the lives of others – that circumstances tend to mirror what you or others focus or obsess about. For instance, I once had a friend who was incredibly fearful of dogs. Every single time I met her for a coffee, sure enough there would be a dog there making her life difficult in some way. I'd meet other friends in exactly the same place and there would no dog in sight, or else a very calm dog.

## ROADBLOCKS

'Your vision will become clear only when you look into your heart. Who looks inside awakens.'

Carl Jung

There are some major roadblocks that you do need to be aware of here. Don't expect to overcome them all overnight as breaking habits formed over a lifetime is going to take time. Just be aware of them because that awareness will gradually work its magic over time to increase the effectiveness of this ritual.

**Confusion:** On the one hand you may be praying (or focusing your intention) for what you want, but at the same time worrying about what you don't want happening or that you aren't being realistic and that it isn't going to work. For example, you may dream of being wealthy but worry that this is a self-centred ideal. If you do that your mind gets confused and can't focus itself to help you take action to achieve your goals. You need to give your mind clear instructions so that it can answer your prayers. Bear in mind that you have thousands of thoughts a day and spending a few moments dreaming of a promotion isn't going to be able to offset the rest of the day worrying what your boss thinks about you. Remember, for prayer to be effective you need to clear out all competing thoughts and believe absolutely in your dreams. You need to eliminate doubt.

**Trivia:** If your life feels small the first place to start looking for reasons why is in your thoughts. Many of our thoughts are repeated from yesterday and the day before and the day before that. Science confirms that many of our thoughts are habitual ones and the great majority of those are trivial and insignificant, like worrying about what someone said, what a celebrity said, what price your bus ticket was and so on.[3] These sort of trivial thoughts can dominate your life, creating feelings of confusion and incompleteness, whereas intention and prayer brings feelings of calm and completeness. If you want to change your life for the better elevate your thoughts to higher and greater things such as, 'What have I got to be grateful for today?' or 'How can I make the world a better place?' Do that kind of thinking often enough and you will soon find the inspiration to take action.

**Competing voices:** Every single day you will be bombarded by the voices and opinions of other people, your family, your culture, your religion and so on. All these voices can make you lose sight of what you want for yourself so you need to find a way to avoid all the competing interference and be single-minded. A few rituals in this book may help you get into a focused state of mind but if all else fails you may want to try a meditation practice to help you to let go of trivial thoughts and find a more detached perspective.

**Your own voice:** Perhaps the biggest roadblock for the power of prayer or intention is the critical voice in your own head that constantly tells you that you can't do something or that you aren't good enough. I'm going to tell you something very important here. None of this negative self-criticism is true but because you think it so often you give it the power of a negative prayer and then this starts manifesting in your life. You need to reprogramme your inner voice so it 'bigs' you up rather than pulls you down.

**Begging rather than believing:** Praying, for the purposes of this book, is not to do with religion – in that you ask or beg God or a higher power (whatever that may mean for you) for help or mercy or comfort. If you beg or ask for something it carries with it the assumption that you have not got it or that it might not be possible. For this ritual to help you change your life you need to operate under the assumption that what you want is or has already happened. For example, if you want to be considered attractive you tell yourself that you are attractive. You know you are attractive. This is a huge leap for many of us – especially if we have low self-esteem – and that is why this ritual comes right after the one on self-love. Remember, if you can't love yourself, success and happiness in life will elude you. It is non-negotiable. From this moment on stop wasting your energy with doubts about yourself and know that you are amazing and that you can have the life of your dreams. If after 21 days you don't see a change in your life you can go back to your old thinking patterns, but for now just give this a try. See what happens!

**Doubts:** If you can't believe something is possible for you it won't manifest in your life so you need to believe it first. Easier said than done if you have got used to thinking you are ordinary but I want to point out here that each one of us is capable of the extraordinary if we just pray and believe. Think of those stories of mothers who summon incredible strength or courage to life heavy objects to save their children's lives or sportsmen that have been written off who win against the odds. What all these people have in common is willpower or the mantra or prayer in their mind that tells them they can do it. Make that your mantra.

## ANECDOTAL EVIDENCE

'Our intention creates our reality.'

Wayne Dyer

There is a real difference between hoping and believing and my writing career has given me proof positive of that recently. Ever since I can remember, my aim as a writer was to empower readers with inspiring and uplifting truths that could make them feel better about their lives. I'm fascinated by all things spiritual and, as a result, have been blessed in having been asked to write book after book in that genre, while also knowing that my work as a writer didn't have mass appeal. Why? Simply because there are a lot of people who don't want to read those types of 'spiritual' books – why should they?

However, I always hoped that one day I would get an opportunity to write an inspiring and potentially life-changing book that would speak to people who wouldn't normally read that sort of thing. I would often ask my publisher about writing a different kind of book to the type I normally write – I even sent in book proposals – but there was never any interest. They saw me as a spiritual writer and I couldn't change that perception. I gave up hope and carried on writing in my comfort zone.

Then six months ago something changed inside me. Perhaps it was a reaction to the turmoil in the world due to religious differences or my children becoming teenagers and saying they knew everything when they clearly didn't and wanting to give them guidance. Whatever it was, I remember waking up in the night and saying to myself out loud, 'I will write a book now that has the potential to speak to everyone and not just the converted few.' I told myself that if no publisher was interested

I would write it and post it on my social media page – which had by now grown so much in popularity it felt like I was being given a sign that the time was right.

I'm not joking, within a week of changing my mind – and believing or praying – I was given the opportunity to write this book. It came out of the blue. It wasn't actually my idea but the inspired idea of my editor, but that didn't matter to me in the slightest. Life was giving me the opportunity to write a life-changing book for anyone that cared to pick it up and that I truly felt I had the experience, knowledge and ability to write.

# PRACTICE: HOW TO PRAY

There is no need to have a separate section explaining how to transform an action into a ritual because prayer is by its very nature a ritual – something sacred with deep personal meaning.

You don't need to be religious to pray and you don't need to go down on bended knee with hands raised unless you want to. All you need to do is use the power of your thoughts to draw what you want into your life. Put as much energy and colour and focus into your thoughts as possible – feel them happening and believe they can happen. Of course, as this book has made clear, just thinking about it isn't enough: you also must take action but setting out your intentions clearly to the universe is the first and most vital step and the solid foundation for everything else that you do to build on it.

If you truly don't know how to pray, or don't want to pray in the way you have done before, please know that there is no right or wrong way. You can speak your beliefs out loud or silently. You can kneel or you can walk. The important thing is that it is personal to you as that will give it sacred meaning. The one thing I would recommend is that you take time out to do it, preferably in peace and quiet, and when you do it you don't just think it but feel it with all your heart. What you are doing is using your positive intention or belief to bring about positive change. You just need a few minutes to focus your mind and your feelings and your energy on what you want to manifest. If you are religious you may want to ask a higher power or God to support you in manifesting your intention. Lighting a candle may also bring a sense of sacredness.

## BRINGING THE RITUAL TO LIFE

'Live your dream. Create your life. Live with Intention.'
Leslie Schwartz

Be as specific as you can and do be realistic with achieving things that you can get your head around. For example, if you want to be a bestselling writer but have never been published before see yourself successfully publishing a few features in your local newspaper or writing a blog first and then, when that goal is achieved, you will have gained the confidence to focus on the next stage of your plan for global literary domination.

This is the one ritual that is an exception to the rest because prayer won't take a few moments but your entire day to complete. In other words during your entire day you focus your thoughts on what you want to happen and – as stressed many times in this section – believe it will happen. See it happening with your thoughts and daydreams and dreams as often as you can for the next 21 days. If you find your mind doubting or being diverted back to trivia or unimportant thoughts gently direct your focus back to the outcome you visualized in Ritual #6 (see page 50).

## FOR THE RECORD

**Life-changing ritual:** What you focus your thoughts on manifests.

**The theory:** By praying for something and focusing on achieving the outcome you can draw it into your life.

**The practice:** Your prayers can be as simple or as complex as you choose, but bring them to mind as you go through the day. Note down any positive changes as a result of adding prayer into your daily routine.

### DO IT: SAY A LITTLE PRAYER!

Of course, positive thinking without action in the real world isn't going to get you anywhere but equally action without positive thinking isn't going to get you anywhere either because you simply won't feel inspired or energized without it. You need to do both. There truly is magical power in focusing your thoughts and intentions, and to expect rather than hope for success. Remember, praying is not about begging or asking, it is about expecting. If you don't like the word 'prayer', substitute 'intention' or 'meditation' instead.

If you don't see any positive changes in your life as a result then feel free to return to your old thinking habits. You have everything to gain by giving this a go and absolutely nothing of value to lose but a negative mind-set.

'By choosing your thoughts and by selecting which emotional currents you release and which you will reinforce you determine the nature of the experiences of your life.'

Gary Zukov

# LIFE-CHANGING RITUAL #**12**

# LIGHT SOMEONE UP

'No act of kindness, no matter how small, is ever wasted.'

Aesop

So far in this book all the focus has quite rightly been on you. Starting your day right, setting and believing in your intentions and loving yourself with all your heart and soul to ensure good things happen to you. For this ritual and the next one, however, the spotlight is turned on other people. The focus will return completely to you after that, because you must be the change you want to see in your world, but for now let's talk about other people.

There is no denying that other people – their opinions, lifestyle and suggestions – will affect you and your life however much you believe in yourself and your dreams. The closer someone is to your heart the more they are likely to impact you, but it is surprising how even a brief interaction with a stranger can sometimes influence your mood or behaviour during the day. Recent research has shown that the human mind is extremely receptive to suggestions, especially if the suggestions were made by people we trust.[1–2]

We don't realize it but we tend to alter our behaviour in order to match people's expectations of us. The key to breaking free from this is, of course, to ignore these expectations and focus on the expectations you have for yourself.

Don't let anyone determine your importance, capabilities or worthiness apart from you, and I hope the previous rituals and the ones that follow will all reinforce the importance of emotional detachment and self-focus. There is, however, another surprising way to break free from the power other people have to influence your life in a negative way: try to help them.

When you help, inspire or are kind to others the recipients of your generosity aren't the only ones to benefit. You will benefit greatly too and increase your chances of success and happiness in life. So Ritual #12 and its companion Ritual #13 encourage you to give something to others. Let's explain why and the benefits to you and how it can change your life for the better.

## THE BENEFITS

> 'The true greatness of a person, in my view, is evident in the way he or she treats those with whom courtesy and kindness are not required.'
>
> Joseph B. Wirthlin

Here are some powerful reasons why helping others makes you feel happier; I hope they will inspire you to give a little:

**The helper's high:** Studies show that when people who do regular volunteer work or give time or items to charity feel-good chemicals are released in the brain.[3-4] This 'helper's high' is experienced not just for good deeds or donation but anytime you do something kind with no thought of personal reward, even if it is something small and relatively insignificant like holding a door open for the person behind you.

**Mood enhancer:** For four weeks researchers at the University of British Columbia assigned people with high anxiety levels to do kind acts for other people.[5] These acts ranged from holding doors open to donating to charity or buying a friend lunch. At the end of the four weeks the researchers found that doing nice things for people led to an increase in people's positive mood and an increase in social confidence.

**Confidence boost:** Studies have also shown that people who do give their time tend to have higher self-esteem – as we have seen, healthy self-esteem is essential for a happy and successful life.[6]

**Perspective shift:** Helping others can change your attitude and boost your mood, making you more optimistic. Doing good or helping others is empowering too and gives you a sense of meaning and purpose.

**Inner peace:** Helping others is a surprising way to ease stress and find a sense of inner calm and peace. It can also make you feel more appreciative of what you already have. Above all, research from the University of Texas showed that helping others empowers you to help yourself.[6]

**The third-party effect:** You helping others doesn't just help you and the person involved: there is another third-party factor. Researchers from the University of Cambridge found that if anyone else sees (or even just hears about) someone being helped it spurs them on to do something good for others. So in this way one good deed really can make the world a better place.[7]

**Getting what you give:** Remember the law of attraction – what you think about tends to manifest in your life (see page 101). It truly is the same with your words and deeds. You get what you give. So if you want to feel loved, try to give others love. If you want help and support, give others help and support. Don't believe me? Try it for just three weeks and see if I'm right. You have nothing to lose but self-absorption.

**People don't forget:** Another compelling benefit of making others feels special is that people tend to remember not what you said or did but how you made them feel and if you have made someone feel better they will feel good about you. People are more likely to help you if you help and support them and are kind to them when they need it. Time and time again in my life I have found when I give to others from the heart I am rewarded by their loyalty and, in some instances, their support, help and advice.

So all things considered, helping others feel good in some way truly is a win–win situation.

## ANECDOTAL EVIDENCE

'Whether one believes in a religion or not, and whether one believes in rebirth or not, there isn't anyone who doesn't appreciate kindness and compassion.'

Dalai Lama

As I was writing this book the powerful impact of this ritual hit me square between the eyes. It came to my attention that one of my books was being heavily plagiarised online. This has happened to me many times in the past and I simply report it to my publisher and move on but this time the words really spoke to me. Although this writer – who for the sake of this anecdote I will refer to by the pseudonym Bob – had clearly taken my writing, he had done a beautiful job presenting it, and seemed to understand and love the book. I don't know why but I decided not to contact my publisher and try to make contact with him instead. It's not something I recommend doing but it was what I did.

I sent Bob a message saying that I had noticed what he was doing and could we enter into a dialogue. I told him I wasn't angry and that what he was doing with my work was, in a way, a kind of compliment. I didn't really expect an answer but within moments I got one. He was deeply apologetic and grateful that I had not reported him. He told me some personal details, which I can't repeat here, and my heart went out to him. I knew he wasn't lying, as it is so easy to disappear without a trace online. He was genuinely sorry and a genuine admirer of my work. Anyway, to cut a long story short I decided to try to help. Bob clearly had vastly superior online skills than me and so I made suggestions on how we could perhaps work together. I also praised what he had done with my book.

A few days later I got the most heart- and spirit-inspiring message ever from Bob. He said that he couldn't believe my willingness to forgive, understand and not take action against him, and it had inspired him to do the same for someone else in his life that was hurting. Bob said it felt good helping someone else and from now on he wanted to be a better person.

Reading that message made me feel good too. Sure, I should have reported him because what he was doing was wrong – and I don't recommend or endorse plagiarising another writer's work – but after I got in touch, Bob took the material down immediately and acknowledged the wrong. I sincerely wonder what would have happened if he had received the harsh, cold threat of legal action instead. He may have simply used the material again under a different name, as has happened before many times.

Again, I'm not recommending this course of action; I am just using it to highlight my point because I can tell you that trying to help someone make better life and work choices felt like a deeply meaningful thing for me to do. It filled Bob with a sense of hope and possibility that I don't think any other course of action would have. It also made me feel that my interactions with him had made a difference and that made me feel good.

## ROADBLOCKS

> 'The best portion of a good man's life is his little, nameless, unremembered acts of kindness and love.'
>
> William Wordsworth

Obviously, it is extremely hard to give to others if you aren't feeling great or happy yourself but just because something is hard does not mean it is impossible. You can and should do it, not just because helping others is the right thing to do but also because, as pointed out in the benefits section, helping others truly does help you in every possible way. If you are feeling extremely negative you will be surprised what a lift it gives you to do good for someone else. Don't believe me? You know what I am going to say. Do something good or helpful or inspiring for someone each day for 21 days and see if it makes a difference in your levels of personal happiness. If it doesn't then you can go back to your life as it was before – but I will still recommend that your bedtime reading be Charles Dickens' *A Christmas Carol*.

If you truly feel so empty inside that you have nothing to give others, remember it doesn't have to be a big or time-consuming act of generosity, something as simple as a smile will do the trick. If you can't summon the energy to smile then you might want to spend some time analysing what the underlying cause might be and take steps to resolve the issue.

You may think that this ritual goes against advice given earlier in the book which urges you to focus more on yourself but it truly doesn't because if you are tuned into your own needs helping others will come naturally to you because you know that it feels good to do so. The only time helping becomes toxic is if you are giving to others at the expense of your own happiness, time and energy. If that is the case you need to remind yourself that you simply can't give to others from an empty cup. Fill your cup first and set healthy boundaries because relationships where one person does all the giving are not healthy relationships: they are toxic ones. You need to understand why you are in a relationship with someone who is giving nothing to you in return and if there is no possibility of that balance being corrected follow the earlier ritual and let go.

Of course, there will be times in your life when you are expected to do all the giving: for example, when a young child is in your care or you are taking care of someone who is physically and mentally vulnerable, and if that is the case it is extremely important for your wellbeing that you balance giving to others with giving to yourself.

## PRACTICE:
## HOW TO LIGHT SOMEONE UP

For the next 21 days, at least once a day you need to consciously try to help or inspire or comfort someone in your life. That person can be a close family member or loved one or it could be someone you barely know or a stranger. How you help them doesn't matter. It could be a big act of generosity, like helping a friend move house, or a small act of kindness like making eye contact with the person at the supermarket checkout and saying thank you. It could simply be a warm smile for no reason. It doesn't matter what it is as long as it makes someone else feel better or lightens or lights up their life in some way.

If you aren't sure how to start here are some suggestions:

- Hold a door open for someone and smile when they walk through.

- Buy a colleague a cup of coffee or make them a cup of tea without being asked.

- When you are driving give way to another driver or pedestrians wanting to cross the road.

- Smile and make eye contact with the person serving you at the till.

- Babysit for a friend so she or he can have some time to herself or himself.

- Visit family members you haven't seen for ages.

- Send a friendly 'how are you' text to someone you have lost contact with.

- Drive a friend to the airport.

- Tip the waiter.

- Genuinely compliment someone.

- Genuinely listen to someone and don't interrupt when they are speaking.

- In a group conversation try to ensure everyone gets air time.

- Donate some clothes or money to charity.

- If you hear unpleasant gossip be the one to say something positive.

- Forgive someone.

- Cut someone some slack.

- Let the person in the supermarket with a few items go ahead of you.

- Give someone a hug.

- Write something nice on someone's update posts on Facebook.

- Hold the elevator door open.

- Empathize.

- Talk to someone at work or college you haven't talked to before.

- Give up your seat on the bus or train.

- Smile when you feel like frowning.

- Help someone struggling with heavy bags or a stroller.

- Give a loved one the benefit of the doubt.

## BRINGING THE RITUAL TO LIFE

'I believe in the magic of kindness. Every act of kindness grows the spirit and strengthens the soul.'

Anonymous

When you do something good for another person you will get that helper's high. When you experience that feeling remind yourself that what you are doing is not just for the good of yourself and the benefit of the other person but also for the whole world. Kindness is contagious, remember. Your act of kindness will inspire the person you helped to help someone else and they in turn will help someone and so on.

In addition, helping out makes others who observe your act of kindness feel good. You may have noticed that if you witness someone giving up their seat on a packed train or bus. It restores your faith in human nature. So, if you tell yourself that you truly are changing the world for the better and making it a more loving and interconnected place every time you do something good for someone else you are giving your act of kindness deep meaning and ritualizing it in the process.

## FOR THE RECORD

**Life-changing ritual:** Light someone up.

**The theory:** Helping others feel better makes you feel good and attracts love, help and kindness into your life.

**The practice:** Notice how doing a good deed lights someone else up and how that makes you feel. You might also like to think about the causes that you feel strongly about: perhaps an ageing relative that needs some domestic help, or a charity. Consider how you might be able to make helping them part of your ritual. Note down whether there is a correlation between your willingness to inspire others and your levels of happiness and success.

## DO IT: LIGHT SOMEONE UP!

This may not be the reason you help others but people who engage in kind acts become happier over time because when you are kind to others you feel good as a person – more optimistic, more moral and more positive – and when you feel good about yourself you are more likely to attract good things and people into your life. It is the principle of like seeking like.

So Ritual #12 is all about finding everyday ways to do something nice for someone and help yourself feel great in the process. It encourages you to leave footprints of kindness wherever you go and to remind yourself that your day, and your life, will just feel happier if you give others a piece of your heart rather than a piece of your mind.

'No one has ever become poor by giving.'

Anne Frank

# LISTEN, REALLY LISTEN

'We have two ears and one mouth, so we should listen more than we say.'

Zeno of Cittium

Listening is very closely linked to Ritual #12 – because if you listen to someone you light up their day – so all the benefits, roadblocks and information given for the previous ritual applies here too. Indeed listening to someone was mentioned in the list of suggested acts of kindness for the last ritual (see page 119) so if you are truly pressed for time some days you can combine Rituals #12 and #13, while Ritual #14 will also help you practise really listening.

However, the act of listening is so very, very powerful that it deserves special mention here as a ritual in its own right.

## THE POWER OF LISTENING

'The word listen contains the same letters as the word silent.'

Alfred Brendall

The reason for this being that the ability to be empathetic is one of the greatest ways to ease someone else's pain and suffering. Having empathy is understanding another's situation from their perspective. It is placing yourself in someone else's shoes without judging. Empathy and learning about someone else's worldview is what saves and heals the human race. Empathy is what makes us human. Empathy is evolution and the key to solving relationship conflicts and all the problems in the world. It moves us to a place of courage and compassion.

If you want to change your world and make the world a better place in the process, there can be no better starting point than empathy and to be empathetic you need to listen to what others are saying to you.

In modern times most of us are so distracted by our own busy lives and thoughts that we rarely listen to what other people are saying. We aren't fully engaged and interrupt or lose concentration far more than we realize. The problem with that is not only does it disrespect or minimize the person we are talking to, and make them feel that what they say doesn't matter to us or isn't enough, we might also miss out on discovering or learning something really important.

## ANECDOTAL EVIDENCE

'Wisdom is the reward you get for a lifetime of listening when you'd have preferred to talk.'

Doug Larson

From my own personal experience I have found that being the quiet one in the group, rather than the life and soul can sometimes be truly empowering. It is incredible what you can learn and how much people will share with you if you just give them your attention rather than your viewpoint.

## PRACTICE: HOW TO LISTEN

For the next 21 days, whenever you have a conversation with someone, fully engage with your mind, your heart and your eyes. Don't fiddle with your mobile phone or think ahead to your reply. Give them your undivided attention. Don't listen for right or wrong or what you want to hear or when you can interrupt to make your point, listen to understand the other, to find common ground, to hear their truth and the inspiration and the soul behind their words.

You may also like to ponder the following quotes about the power of listening by perhaps writing them down on a sticky note and placing in a prominent place as a reminder or making part of a mantra or affirmation.

'It takes two to speak the truth – one to speak and another to hear.'

Henry David Thoreau

'The quieter you become the more you can hear.'

Ram Dass

'When you talk you are only repeating what you already know. But if you listen you may learn something new.'

Anonymous

## BRINGING THE RITUAL TO LIFE

'Most people do not listen with the intent to understand; they listen with the intent to reply.'

Stephen Covey

There is sacred power in listening too. It has a deep impact on others, as it makes them feel that what they have to say or contribute matters and it can also have a transforming impact on you. As you enter into different conversations during the day tune into how you are rating as a listener. Are you engaged or have your thoughts wondered? Are you being empathetic or distant?

Become aware of how you paying attention actually impacts the person speaking. You will be surprised how much it can inspire and empower them and if you make others feel good in this way they will in turn feel good around you. You will also be surprised how much you can learn. Study after study has shown that listening is crucial to leadership effectiveness and success in life.[1] See what happens and listen for the gold in what others have to say. It might just be the gold you were hoping to find at the end of your rainbow.

# LIFE-CHANGING RITUAL #14

# RIGHT HERE, RIGHT NOW

'Life is available only in the present moment. If you abandon the present moment you cannot live the moments of your daily life deeply.'

Thich Nhat Hanh

Many of us rush through our days without fully living. We focus so much on our future and what we hope to achieve then – and in some ways this book has encouraged you to do that by making you think about your goals and how to achieve them – but that should never take away from the fact that the only reality is right here and right now – the present moment. The only life you have is happening now and if you aren't paying attention and finding joy and meaning in the present moment then you aren't living your life to the full and a life not lived to the full is not a happy or successful one.

The way to live each day to the full is to be mindful. Mindfulness is the practice of focusing your attention on the present moment – and accepting it without judgement. This isn't as easy as it sounds but if you complete the rituals in this book for the next three weeks you will be well on your way to making mindfulness your way of living. You see, in different ways all the rituals in this book encourage you to appreciate the present moment (because a ritual by definition is something that you must perform with awareness) but this one – the final one to complete during your daytime activities – will reinforce all the others by turning the spotlight brightly on mindfulness. The more appreciative you are of the present moment the better your day will be and the more good days you have the more likely you are to attract success and happiness your way.

## THE BENEFITS

'Living in the moment means letting go of the past and not waiting for the future. It means living your life consciously, aware that each moment you breathe is a gift.'

Oprah Winfrey

Mindfulness has been extensively researched by scientists and found to be a key element of happiness.[1] The practice is very much associated with Buddhism but it transcends religion because it is all about focusing your attention on the present moment and the bigger picture of your life, rather than getting distracted by the details.

Professor emeritus Jon Kabat-Zinn, founder of the stress reduction clinic at the University of Massachusetts Medical Centre was largely responsible for bringing mindfulness into medical practice and showing that it can boost wellbeing. Zinn demonstrated that mindfulness can improve physical health in that it relieves stress, lowers blood pressure, reduces pain and improves sleep. It can also play a part in easing depression, addiction, eating disorders and anxiety disorders.[2]

It is thought by some that this is because mindfulness encourages people to accept their emotions, even painful ones, rather than try to avoid them. For this reason, mindfulness meditation is increasingly prescribed by psychotherapists for helping people deal with negative and destructive thoughts.

Above all, though, research has shown that mindfulness can improve wellbeing. It helps you enjoy or savour life more.[3] People who concentrate on the here and now are less likely to feel anxiety about the future or regret about the past and have greater self-esteem and relationship satisfaction.

## ANECDOTAL EVIDENCE

'I have realized that the past and future are real illusions, that they exist in the present, which is what there is, and all there is.'

Alan Watts

For decades I lived my life on fast forward. I was one of those people who always looked ahead to the next big event or milestone. It was as though I was permanently waiting for something better to happen than right now. I was always in a state of perpetual anticipation.

I used to think that once I was slimmer, or wealthier, or married, or a mother, or a bestselling author, or my children were older, or I had more personal time and so on, my life would really begin. What I didn't realize was that my life had begun the moment I was born and I was wasting it living my present in a state of preparation. It took me close to five decades to truly value the present moment and the catalyst for that leap in my personal development was my children suddenly not being children anymore.

Many wise people told me to enjoy my children while I could but as so often happens when you are given profound advice it falls on deaf ears until you are ready to hear it. When they were young it truly felt as if the childhood phase would never end and I was forever looking ahead and planning the next step in our lives. Then suddenly their childhood was over. One instant I was their world and the next they were teenagers, no longer interested in mum but out there creating their own world.

My children's transition from children to adults was, of course, perfectly natural but I just wasn't prepared for it. I missed my babies terribly. I searched in my mind for memories to comfort me and realized that the only times that truly stood out were holidays and the reason was that I was fully present then with all the other distractions removed. When they were born I looked ahead to their first birthday, and then to when they went to school and then senior school and so on. All the time I was missing the magic of loving and living with them in the moment because I always had the 'it will be better when this or that happens' mind-set.

Sometimes I wish I could go back and soak up each moment of my precious time with my children and not wish it away but then I realize that regret is just as much a waste of the present moment as being distracted by the future. I don't want to make the same mistakes again and waste any more of my precious life not fully appreciating the now. It is still a work in progress for me to live in the present but thankfully I have made great progress with mindfulness practice.

A friend of mine introduced me to the concept a few years ago and I can honestly say it has changed my life for the better. These techniques have finally helped me grasp the idea that today isn't preparation for tomorrow or regret for the past. Today is all that there is, all that I have. Today is the main event. I sincerely hope none of you reading this book will take as long as I did to stop living your life as if you are preparing for something later, but appreciate the right here and right now.

I truly believe that if you can do that you have discovered the secret of true happiness and success in life.

## ROADBLOCKS

'Past and present are in the mind only – I am now.'
Sri Nisargadatta Maharaj

When your mindfulness or ability to be aware of the present moment increases you will find that levels of joy and peace in your life increase. Being familiar with how your mind works makes you feel and live better and happier but there are obstacles. I have wanted to give up on many occasions because truly living in the present isn't easy but as with any challenge overcome the rewards are amazing. The best way to move forward with your right here, right now approach is to know what the potential roadblocks are and to plan how best to deal with them.

First of all know that there will be distractions – they could be negative thoughts, people or tasks demanding your attention, noise and so on. When these happen – and I say when here not if, because they will – see them as opportunities to practise being aware – and even more important, non judgemental – to help you become stronger. The challenges you face are teachers in disguise and they will help you grow.

Second, you need to understand that when you start mindfulness your thoughts will be all over the place. You will often feel that this is hopeless but the crucial thing here is to persist through the chaos because, trust me here, the more you practise, the easier it gets and if you practice appreciating the now during everyday tasks it will become easier and easier for you.

Third, you will find that there will be times when you just want to give up because you don't feel you are making any progress. Try to remind yourself during these times that this is the darkness before the dawn and it is often the case that when you feel you are getting nowhere you are actually close to a breakthrough. Don't give up – certainly not for 21 days at least.

Fourth, negative emotions or feelings of anxiety, anger, stress and frustration will be your biggest roadblock. When they strike, and they will, acknowledge them but don't judge them as good or bad. Just notice them and let them go. You also need to understand that whenever you feel emotions like that you are not living in the present moment but being pulled forward by the future or dragged back by the past. In addition, when negative thoughts and emotions strike, the chances are you are allowing other people or your plans to be responsible for your wellbeing and happiness and this is a recipe for disaster as the only person who can make you truly happy is you. Mindfulness will return you to centre stage where you belong.

Fifth, if you feel like you aren't making any progress with mindfulness try to remind yourself that there is no goal here. The journey is the destination. Whenever you practise mindfulness you are focusing on the here and now and in the process you are learning and growing. You are already at your destination.

Finally, there will be a part of you that doesn't want to be in the here and now, especially if you are having to deal with difficult emotions or situations. If that is the case remind yourself that you are learning to accept what is – because that is all that there is. The only way to feel good is to find joy and peace right here right now, as this quote by Eckhart Tolle says far better than I can:

> 'Unease, anxiety, tension, stress, worry – all forms of fear – are caused by too much future and not enough presence. Guilt, regret, resentment, grievances, sadness, bitterness and all forms of non-forgiveness are caused by too much past, and not enough presence.'
>
> Eckhart Tolle

# PRACTICE: HOW TO BE MORE MINDFUL

Anything you do can be transformed into a mindfulness ritual, whether it's drinking a cup of tea (see page 82) or listening to another person speak (see page 123), if you give it your full attention. Remember, mindfulness is about focusing entirely on what you are doing with care and joy and not being distracted by other things.

You may also find the following suggestions helpful in bringing this ritual into your life:

**Walk with awareness:** When you walk somewhere, pay attention to each step. Listen to your breathing, your heartbeat and observe everything around you.

**Single tasking:** At some point in your day choose one task and give it your complete attention for whatever time you can. Don't switch your focus to anything else. As you brush your teeth, eat a banana, drive your car, walk, shower or do other everyday activities, be fully present and involve all your senses. Bring your attention to the sensations in your body in the present moment. Notice each sight, touch and sound so you can savour every sensation.

**Look for beauty:** Each day find someone or something and see the beauty, only the good, in them or it. Perhaps there is a willow tree on your way to work or a picture in your office or a street that you walk down that you know but haven't really noticed. Notice and appreciate every detail.

**Clean up:** At some point in your day you are going to wash your hands or wash something up. Do it while paying careful attention to the water and the soap.

**Listen to the sound of silence:** Find a few moments each day to be completely silent with no televisions, mobiles or computers nearby.

**Immerse yourself in a good book:** It may seem that reading is a way of moving your mind away from the present to another place but if you pay all your attention to what you are reading it is a wonderful way to find your focus.

**Allow emotions:** If you feel angry or anxious or guilty or sad during the day don't try to avoid those feelings: just become aware of that emotion and let it be present without judgement of whether what you are feeling is good or bad. Then let that emotion go. You can also practise this technique for cravings (addictive substances or behaviours). Notice the craving, don't judge it and know that in time it will pass.

**Watch your thoughts:** Spend a few moments just watching what thoughts come into your mind. Notice what thoughts make you feel good and which ones have the opposite effect. Don't get caught up with the past or future, just watch your thoughts as they are right now.

## BRINGING THE RITUAL TO LIFE

'A monk told Joshu, "I have just entered the monastery. Please teach me."
Joshu asked, "Have you eaten your rice porridge."
The monk replied, "I have eaten."
Joshu said, "Then you had better wash your bowl."
At that moment the monk was enlightened.'

Zen story

Being mindful is a ritual because it is something you do that has deep meaning and whenever you focus on the present moment you are giving that present moment deep meaning.

Ritual isn't about doing a routine or activity mindlessly. It's a way of building something good and deeply meaningful and empowering into your life. If you aren't mindful during all the rituals in this book they are meaningless, so I hope the right here, right now ritual suggestions on pages 133–5 will not only encourage a more mindful approach to your daily life but reinforce all the other rituals in this book. All 21 daily rituals should be performed with deep reverence for, and awareness of, the present moment.

## FOR THE RECORD

**Life-changing ritual:** Every day make sure you find time to be right here, right now.

**The theory:** Appreciating the present moment fully is a way of living that increases your chances of happiness significantly.

**The practice:** When you practice mindfulness, you may find that your breathing slows down and you become more meditative, as your body and mind feels calmer, and your thoughts less intrusive. As you spend more time in the present moment, observe how it also affects your ability to stay calm in a crisis and weather stressful situations when they happen. Notice where there is a correlation between your ability to focus on the here and now and your levels of happiness and success.

## DO IT: RIGHT HERE, RIGHT NOW!

More than anything, being mindful involves accepting whatever arises in your awareness at any given moment, whether it is positive or negative. It involves you being kind and gentle with yourself. If your mind wanders into criticism, judgement or distraction, simply slow down and redirect it gently back to your present moment.

The more you are able to savour your experiences and be aware of the present moment without judging, the simpler it becomes to accept whatever comes your way during the rest of the day. And the easier it will be for you to make the most of your day and every day, and in the process dramatically change your entire life for the better.

'Stop acting as if life is a rehearsal. Live this day as if it were your last. The past is over and gone. The future is not guaranteed... but you have right now.'

Wayne Dyer

# DAILY CHECK POINT

At some point during the day review the seven rituals below to make sure you have completed them all. For ease of reference you may want take a photograph of this list on your mobile phone or quickly jot them down on a piece of paper and fix to your desk or wall.

**Ritual #8: Tidy one thing**

**Ritual #9: Say a little prayer**

**Ritual #10: Let it go**

**Ritual #11: Fill your own cup**

**Ritual #12: Light someone up**

**Ritual #13: Listen, really listen**

**Ritual #14: Right here, right now**

# PART III

# RETIRE WITH SATISFACTION
# 7 LIFE-CHANGING EVENING RITUALS

'A well spent day brings happy sleep.'

Leonardo da Vinci

The seven remaining rituals of your day should be performed every evening after you have finished your daily routine or as you are winding down the activities of your day. I'm going to call this time, when most of us prepare for bed and wave goodbye to the day, your magic or golden time because what you do in that time is crucial not just for a refreshing sleep but also to help you wake up in a positive frame of mind the next day. It is also the time of the day when you gently wind down and that will be reflected in the reduction of information presented for you to process, with one or two pages now for each ritual and the amount of text decreasing.

All seven of the rituals that follow are gentle and so simple, easy and natural to perform that little explanation is required, and you'll notice that they contain a loss less information that the previous ones. I truly believe that at this point in the book, after reading all the previous rituals, you will be at a stage of increased awareness now and be able to intuitively sense or grasp the benefits and potential of each suggested ritual to change your life for the better. In other words, no explanation is required because deep down somewhere you will just know they will benefit you enormously.

When was the last time you were genuinely happy at the end of the day and retired to bed feeling pleased with yourself? Perhaps it was when you did something that made you feel proud of yourself or reached a goal you had set for yourself? Perhaps it was when you had simply spent a day doing things you love and seeing people you love? Or perhaps it was when you had a day that you felt made a difference?

Whatever the reasons you felt satisfied I want you to remember how it felt to end your day on a high note. This book is all about encouraging you to live each day to the full so that when it comes to the end of the day you can truly retire with genuine satisfaction, knowing that you had the best day ever and that when you wake up the next morning it will once again be with great determination.

# LIFE-CHANGING RITUAL #**15**

# OVER TO YOU

'The best thinking has been done in solitude.'

Thomas Edison

We are repeatedly and rightly told that there are so many benefits to our health and happiness from positive relationships and social interaction with others rather than being alone, but Ritual #15 is going to balance all that and ask you to ensure that having completed your tasks, you spend some time alone. It doesn't matter how long, but a minimum of 10 minutes' alone time is suggested preferably every evening to give you a chance to reflect on the day.

## THE BENEFITS

'Without great solitude no serious work is possible.'

Pablo Picasso

An emerging body of research is suggesting that, if done in the right way, some time alone each day can be extremely beneficial and life enhancing. The research even suggests that even the most extravert and socially orientated people should still spend some time in solitude if they want to improve their focus and creative thinking and have fully rounded personalities.[1] In short, just as regular exercise and healthy eating can make us feel better, so can regular time alone.

This makes sense because for centuries solitude has been linked to creativity, empowerment and intellectual breakthroughs in the lives of great religious leaders, artists, scientists, innovators and musicians. Some of the best and most brilliant ideas happen in solitude. Despite this, many of us associate solitude with deprivation or feeling bad or blue but in moderation solitude is essential for finding out what you really think.

All too often our judgement or thinking is clouded by the opinions or expectations of others and, while you should always take on board what others think and learn from it if we can, we should also learn to trust our own instinct or intuition and you simply can't do that in a group. You need to do that alone.

There truly is great power in peace and solitude. During that time you return to your centre and recalibrate your sense of self. For me, solitude is a vital ingredient for a successful day and life. It is the time to listen to my thoughts and to reflect on events and to simply be. I take stock and tune into what is vital to my wellbeing.

And perhaps the more practical benefit of taking some time away from the hustle and bustle of life – whether that's other family members or roommates or simply the sound of the blaring TV or domestic appliances rumbling – is that it helps us to wind down and relax, which is important if we are to sleep well later.

## ANECDOTAL EVIDENCE

'One can be instructed in society, one is inspired only in solitude.'

Gary Mark Gilmore

Solitude is something that has always been incredibly important to me and when my husband was at work all day and my children at school I cherished my time alone, writing, thinking and dreaming.

Five years ago my husband took early retirement and suddenly I wasn't on my own during the day any longer. At first it was wonderful to have the company but after a while I started to get irritable for no reason, especially with the two dogs my husband brought into our household, as they constantly fought with my two cats. Add into that mix two teenage children with what seemed to be endless study leave from school and it all got a bit overwhelming.

I managed to survive though and I did that by giving myself permission to hide away for a while every evening in my office. I would lock my door and just enjoy the bliss of being entirely alone. In that time I would listen to music or close my eyes and not sleep but recharge, or simply sit and dream. I'm convinced that if I hadn't insisted on that 'me' time I would have 'lost the plot'.

# PRACTICE:
# HOW TO BE ALONE

There is too much anxiety surrounding the idea of solitude for many people today but being on your own can be very liberating and empowering. In an age when mobiles offer us instant connection even when we are alone the actual definition of alone is vague, but for the purpose of this book it is simply spending a minimum of 10 minutes alone every day away from anyone else, with your phone switched off or in another room.

If this simply isn't possible because you live in a busy and occupied home then you need to find some 'alone together' time when you go for a walk outside by yourself or a trip to a coffee bar by yourself, take a shower or hang a 'do not disturb' sign on your bedroom door and, if necessary, pop in some earplugs. The important thing is that regardless of external circumstances this is something you do alone – and, even more important, you leave your mobile behind or only respond to an emergency call, not to texts or emails or messages.

You may find that when you do this over the next 21 days – even if you limit your alone time to just 10 minutes – that you may feel slightly anxious or unhappy by yourself. That is perfectly natural if you are used to always being around other people. Just observe, don't judge, those uncomfortable feelings and take your time out because studies show that even if your alone time is not particularly happy there seems to be some kind of rebound effect and you will experience more positive emotions and greater confidence and self-worth over the days and weeks ahead as a result.

## BRINGING THE RITUAL TO LIFE

'Solitude is the great teacher and to learn its lessons you must pay attention to it.'

Deepak Chopra

In order to get something out of your alone time make it clear to yourself that taking time out by yourself is your choice and then give that time alone great meaning (ritualize it) by reminding yourself that this time is your time to forge a clearer identity and direction that is yours and yours alone. Solitude is not the same as loneliness. Loneliness is a wretched feeling that something is missing but those who can enjoy solitude discover their own inner depth and this inner depth helps them focus and be creative. Spending time alone can also make you more capable of empathy and better social interaction as it gives you a break from constantly being available and much needed time to recharge.

### DO IT: OVER TO YOU!

If you are a fan of Jane Austin's immortal novels you will be familiar with the heroine's regular need to take time out to reflect on the day's events in her room and how these reflections help her grow in understanding and as a person. So, for the next 21 days treat yourself to some daily alone time at the end of your busy day to reflect on what has been, all that is and all that could be. Seek out the life-changing gift of solitude.

The mind is sharper and keener in seclusion and uninterrupted solitude. Originality thrives in seclusion, free of outside influences beating upon us to cripple the creative mind.

'Be alone – that is the secret of invention: be alone, that is where ideas are born.'

Nikola Tesla

# LIFE-CHANGING RITUAL #**16**

# SAY GRACE

'All great change... begins at the dinner table.'

Ronald Reagan

At some point in your evening you are going to eat. Most of us tend to rush or even skip lunch or eat on the go during our busy days but this ritual is all about making your evening meal feel meaningful. Saying Grace before a meal is not about religion. It is about an attitude of gratitude for your meal and respect for yourself and others. For example, you might choose to be grateful for the simple fact of having food on your plate when so many in the world do not, or for the producers that have grown the vegetables, or the lorry drivers that brought it the grocery store, and so on. In this way, saying Grace not only brings some sacredness to your evening meal but also becomes an act of mindfulness (see page 127) in itself.

## THE BENEFITS

'The most essential part of my day is a proper dinner.'

Rachael Ray

Taking time to savour your food and to bring a sense of meaning to your evening meal has many benefits. Scientists have shown that families who enjoy their family dinners together are closer, argue and divorce less and have children and teenagers who do better at school; they also are less likely to be smoking, drinking and taking drugs or suffer depression and anxiety.[1] This isn't surprising as the family meal is an important time for a family to bond and foster a sense of belonging. It is the family glue.

For those who live alone suppertime can also be a positive and sacred time. This meal is about you being your best friend and taking the best care of yourself because you are worth it. Remember, people who know they are worth it have happier and more successful lives than people who don't take care of themselves so see your evening meal as an opportunity to show yourself just how much you care about you.

Whether you dine with others or alone, saying Grace, or doing something similar like lighting a candle, is a cue to remind your body to stop running around and slow down to eat and digest a healthy and nutritious meal. Time to eat therefore becomes a time to focus on your food and give your body the quality nourishment and fuel it needs to function at its peak.

## ANECDOTAL EVIDENCE

'The dinner table is the heart of the home.'

Anonymous

These days I consciously make a decision to make my evening meal memorable. The reason I make this decision is because about 10 years ago my children told me something I sort of knew but didn't want to admit to myself – they told me that I was a terrible cook. From then on it became a running joke in our family that people better prepare themselves for a taste disaster when I was cooking and they were probably right.

Initially, I found it amusing but after a while the joke turned stale and I kind of gave up. As the years passed by I started to rely heavily on takeaways and the evening meal became a rushed and stressed affair, as increasingly the takeaway would arrive too early or too late. Then when she was about 14 my lovely daughter found within herself a passion for cooking and she gradually started to take over the evening meal. She did a beautiful job and dinner times were happy times of connection, something they hadn't been before.

I do feel a bit ashamed as a mother narrating this story but also proud of my daughter because she taught me the importance of giving the evening meal meaning. It was not so much what she cooked – as many of her meals were very simple, with beans on toast being her speciality – it was the sense of sacredness she brought back to our meals. How did she do that? She did it in a very simple way. She absolutely insisted on lighting a candle before the evening meal.

The simple act of lighting a candle brought a sense of sacredness to the meal and gave me and everyone in my family a chance to focus on our food and being together.

You'll be glad to hear that my daughter is busy with her friends most evenings now and I have returned to the position of head chef but, even if I am eating alone or ordering a takeaway, I have never forgotten what she taught me. I light a candle. It slows me down and gives my meal meaning.

# PRACTICE:
# SIMPLE SUPPER RITUALS

There is an emotional and spiritual aspect to eating with a sense of reverence. Lighting a candle is a powerful way to bring focus and sacredness into being at the table. However, you don't have to light a candle to achieve that – you can simply create a beautiful centre piece to your table to concentrate attention, such as a bunch of flowers or an unusual ornament or some inspiring artwork.

Religious or not, you could also say Grace to help bring gratitude and meaning to your meal. You might choose a traditional spiritual or religious blessing or make up your own secular blessing. In fact, saying Grace can be as simple as saying, for example, 'Thank you for bringing us home safely today and for this time together and the food on our plates.'

If saying Grace doesn't appeal to you then raise your glasses to say 'bon appetite' or simply bring blessings. Reading poetry or even singing a song or listening to music are other rituals you might like to include. If you live with other people or with your family then try to ensure everyone sits around the table.

If you have a family or live with room-mates, it may be that conversation sometimes become heated over dinner and perhaps ends in disagreement. If that's the case then you might like to agree to stick to lighter topics of conversations. If you stray into conversational territory that's likely to cause tension then perhaps agree a phrase beforehand, such as 'back in the here and now' or 'tomatoes and sausages', which reminds everyone to let the subject go and simply enjoy eating together.

## BRINGING THE RITUAL TO LIFE

'After a good dinner one can forgive anybody, even one's own relations.'

Oscar Wilde

If you live alone why not invite friends over at least once or twice a week to give your meals a sense of occasion? If that's not possible be sure to sit down and bring a sense of meaning to your meal too – perhaps combining it with the Ritual #15 (see page 141). Use the time to savour your food and the events of the day and to give yourself some loving self-care.

Living together or alone, keep supper sacred by sitting down, or giving everyone time to get seated, before starting to eat (that includes the person who has cooked the meal). Don't allow mobile phones or other devices at the table and make sure that the TV is switched off. Eat slowly and with awareness. Use cutlery and fine china if you can and after your meal has finished take a few moments to sit quietly before rushing to clear everything away.

You might also like to end your meal by thanking the person who cooked it or the producers that helped bring the food to your plate.

## DO IT: SAY GRACE!

Your evening meal ritual does not have to be saying Grace, or to be what you were familiar with when you were a child. It does not have to be complicated or time consuming and can simply be a moment of silence before you eat. Whatever ritual you choose the important thing is that it is meaningful to you. It brings a sense of gratitude and appreciation and helps ensure that for the next 21 days your evening meal is nutritious, pleasurable and, most important of all, truly sacred.

'Grace isn't a little prayer you say before receiving a meal. It's a way to live.'

Anonymous

# LIFE-CHANGING RITUAL #**17**

# WRITE IT DOWN

'Daydreaming had started me on the way but writing once
I was truly in its grip took me and shook me awake.'

Eudora Welty

Journaling at the end of each day is an extremely powerful
ritual. It's not about keeping a secret diary as many teenagers
do but a mindful practice that truly can improve your life.
Writing things down can help you understand your day
better and also be an outlet for creative expression. Many of
us type a lot of comments on social media but our energy
might be better spent if we keep an offline journal that really
speaks our minds and comments on what really is happening
in our lives, not on what we think our friends or followers
want to read.

## THE BENEFITS

'Journal writing is a voyage to the interior.'

Christina Baldwin

Apart from the obvious benefit of journal writing being a permanent reminder of your personal history that you can reflect on whenever you want, it is also a way to track your progress in all areas of your life. Research also shows that journaling that takes into account your future goals increases your likelihood of achieving them because it gives you an opportunity to see if your daily tasks are in line with your long-term vision.[1] It seems that the act of writing down your goals somehow increases your chances of achieving them, perhaps because when you write something down it feels more official and helps your mind focus.

University of Texas at Austin psychologist James Pennebaker has also confirmed that not only can journaling ease stress and boost immunity but also it can help you come to terms with difficult events. Creative writing involves both your analytical and logical left brain and your intuitive right brain and therefore allows you to use all your brain power to understand yourself better and the world around you.[2] Last, but by no means least, journaling is an opportunity for you to end your day knowing that you did the best you could and this creates motivation and momentum for the following day.

## ANECDOTAL EVIDENCE

'Keep a daily diary of your dreams, goals, and accomplishments. If your life is worth living, it's worth recording.'

Marilyn Grey

Did you ever keep a secret diary when you were a child? I know I did. I had one of those magical five-year ones with a lock and a key, and I managed to fill about two years of it consistently but then when I hit my late teenage years with all its distractions keeping a dairy lost its appeal. I recently reread my diary and found it to be incredibly revealing about the adult I was to become. I did not realize it at the time but what I was doing was questioning and challenging myself and in some cases coming up with profound answers.

It took several decades for me to revisit journaling and the catalyst for doing that was a magazine feature I was asked to write on its benefits. I discovered that it was a vital tool for transformation for self-help icon Tony Robbins and that it is also a ritual that many highly successful people live by. As I researched and wrote that feature it became abundantly clear to me that this was one ritual that would truly benefit my life it I incorporated it into my day. I was right. My day feels incomplete – and is incomplete – if I haven't written something down about what I felt and thought about the day and how I can do better tomorrow.

## PRACTICE: HOW TO JOURNAL

To get started you just need a pen and paper or, better still, a notebook, or if you prefer digital, your phone, tablet, laptop or PC. To make the experience as successful a ritual as possible keep it very simple and focus your thoughts on just two questions:

1. What did I learn about myself and others today?

2. What can I do to make tomorrow even better than today?

Then for the next 21 days write down your answers. You may write one sentence or dozens of sentences – it doesn't matter how little or how long you spend journaling, the crucial thing is that at some point in your evening you articulate your thoughts in writing about the two questions above. Some days if you are pressed for time you may simply prefer to speak into the recorder of your mobile phone and that's fine as long as you focus your words on the two questions above. Try to answer as honestly as you can.

If some things feel hard to write or say and share with yourself refer to yourself in the third person. We all have dark days sometimes. Don't feel that you always have to be bright and upbeat in your journal all the time because then it would not be honest and the true power of journaling lies in its honesty. Use your journal time to explore this darkness instead and release difficult problems and emotions and you might find light within yourself as you do.

You may be wondering if social media, Facebook, Twitter and so on, is equivalent to journaling and my recommendation here would be to keep your journaling separate from all that unless you truly feel ready to share with your friends the secrets and mysteries of your inner world. As you'll see in the next ritual – higher selfie – I'm not actually against social media and I think if used wisely it can actually be extremely positive but for this ritual I would strongly urge privacy. For a true sense of self there are some things that should be kept sacred and personal to you and to you alone. If you share everything about yourself with others you run the risk of completely losing yourself in others. You are like a reed blown in the wind.

## BRINGING THE RITUAL TO LIFE

'The more light you allow within you, the brighter the world you live in will be.'

Shakti Gawain

Journaling reminds you that powerful people with a sense of strong identity have that inner strength because there is a part of themselves that they keep private or just for them. They don't need validation from others for absolutely everything they say, do and think. They know and trust their own mind, heart and spirit.

Journaling is a ritual with deep personal meaning because it helps you learn about yourself and when you learn about yourself you grow. It is about paying attention to what is within you for the purpose of living well from the inside out. To make it a successful ritual commit to the practice for a minimum of three weeks and keep your focus on the two questions listed above, as they are extremely effective in helping you grow personally.

**DO IT: WRITE IT DOWN!**

You don't have to be a writer to keep a journal – remember it has been proven to improve clarity and perspective and to reduce stress, as well as being a key ingredient in achieving goals successfully. In short, journaling is an amazing personal-development tool and when combined with all the other rituals in this book it can significantly increase your overall wellbeing and levels of happiness, success and enlightenment.

'I write because I don't know what I think until I read what I say.'

Flannery O'Connor

# LIFE-CHANGING RITUAL #**18**

# HIGHER SELFIE

'When you possess light within you see it externally.'

Anaïs Nin

The ability to look yourself in the eye and tell yourself you are beautiful or handsome is a powerful yet simple action you can do to change your life for the better. You see, once you are able to accept and appreciate yourself fully a shift within you happens. People sense or reflect your inner confidence and you naturally start to attract better things into your life.

## THE BENEFITS

'A happy person is a beautiful person.'

Anonymous

Billions are spent on beauty products and treatments each year, yet despite the steep price tag for our pursuit of beauty most people only experience a temporary boost in self-confidence as a result, causing them to pay even more and the cycle continues. Keeping up with the totally unrealistic idea of beauty created by airbrushing is a futile goal that will result in disappointment, lack of self-worth and reduction in funds.

Building your self-esteem is a far cheaper way to feel attractive and research even backs up the inside-out approach to beauty by showing that people with good self-esteem have happier lives with greater chances of success in life compared to people who don't like themselves or consider themselves unattractive.[1] In other words, the happier you are, the more likely it is you will feel attractive and appear attractive to others.

## ANECDOTAL EVIDENCE

'Beauty is not in the face; beauty is a light in the heart.'
Kahlil Gibran

Have you ever met someone you thought was beautiful but when you get to know them, they don't seem so attractive anymore? In much the same way, have you met someone who you didn't initially think was very attractive but over time as you get to know them they become more and more attractive. This has happened to me more times than I can remember and it has never ceased to fascinate me.

Something else that I have noticed too is that if you honestly compliment someone this can actually have a transformative impact on their appearance. Don't believe me? Try it and see. Tell someone you think their outfit is flattering or their haircut amazing or that they have a wonderful smile and watch how it makes them glow. You may also notice that they wear the same outfit again and again or smile more. You will see them grow taller. Many times when I was a fitness instructor I saw my clients becoming more beautiful before my eyes. It wasn't just their exercise routine – although that, of course, played a part – it was also their growing confidence, as I told them that they looked great – and it was true: I could literally see their potential for inner beauty or power growing. Within each one of us there is the potential to be drop-dead gorgeous but we simply don't believe in it. Beauty starts from within. When you believe from within that you are beautiful, when you focus on what is positive and strong inside you, then that inner beauty will reflect in your appearance. You will also naturally take care of yourself better and do all the things that can enhance your external beauty. There is absolutely no point, however, focusing only on the external because true beauty can only come from the inside out.

## PRACTICE: HOW TO TAKE YOUR HIGHER SELFIE

You'll already know from the other rituals that every choice we make – from what we say and think and feel to what we eat and how much we exercise – creates true beauty from the inside out. The best way to grow in beauty from the inside out is to accept and love yourself, but how do you do that? Every self-help book and spiritual tradition advises self-love but rarely do they tell us how to go about it. This book, however, is going to give you a self-love ritual that is incredibly powerful. For the next 21 days, in the evening when you are relaxing and preferably after you have completed your journal, you are going to take a photograph of yourself, a selfie. You can post that photo on your social media or you can just keep it on your phone.

When you take your selfie look yourself right in the eye and think about how far you have come and all the love and goodness in your spirit. Smile broadly at yourself and mentally tell yourself how grateful you are for you. Flirt with your own reflection. Imagine you are meeting the person of your dreams and need to make a good impression. Then take a photo. Do a retake or two if you feel you could pose in a more flattering way. This is going to feel uncomfortable at first but the benefits are immeasurable. After you have taken your photo look for what you admire and appreciate about yourself in that photo. If you can't find anything look again. You are losing perspective totally. There will be something there because, trust me, there always is.

## BRINGING THE RITUAL TO LIFE

'To me there is nothing more beautiful than inner peace in a man or woman.'

Alice Greczyn

To turn this into a ritual you need to see this as so much more than simply taking a photo. It has absolutely nothing to do with vanity and everything to do with discovering your own inner power or beauty. As you progress through the 21 days

I would also like you to refer back to photos and see how, as you grow in confidence and happiness, your appearance starts to change. Compare the photo you took on day 1 with the photo on day 7 and then the photo on day 7 with the photo on day 14 and then 21. You will see that you grow in beauty.

If you can't quite believe what I'm saying here I'd like to point you in the direction of some research which seems to suggest that the happier you are from the inside the more attractive you will look.[2] It seems that your facial features will harmonize as an outer reflection of that inner peace.[3-5] So when you take your own photo over the next 21 days you really could be keeping an external record of your inner state, or higher selfie.

## DO IT: HIGHER SELFIE!

We live in a selfie-obsessed culture so this ritual is asking you to take something typically considered vain and thoughtless and transform it into something quite wonderful. Taking your photo every day is about you appreciating and celebrating what is beautiful and powerful within you. The more you focus on your own strength and your own beauty and accept who you are, rather than comparing yourself with others or demanding impossible standards of perfection from yourself, the more you will glow with beauty and power from the inside out.

'Life is like a camera. Focus on what's important. Capture the good times. Develop from the negatives, and if things don't work out take another shot.'

Anonymous

# LIFE-CHANGING RITUAL #**19**

# REPEAT AFTER ME

'It's the repetition of affirmations that lead to belief. And once that belief becomes a deep conviction, things begin to happen.'

Muhammed Ali

Would you believe me if I told you that one single statement repeated for three weeks in row has the potential to plant a seed in your mind which, if constantly nourished by the other 20 rituals in this book, can develop into your reality? Of course, as I described in the introduction to this book (see page ix) thoughts without actions won't work but upgrading your thinking is a powerful way to supercharge your efforts, and this ritual will show how positive thinking can encourage and attract positive change.

Of course, I do hope that by now you will have opened your mind to the powerful realization that you really can change your life for the better by changing your daily routine. I do hope you will also know without a shadow of doubt that the only person who can make that positive change is you, by taking charge of your thoughts and then taking appropriate action in your daily life. The person you are right now has been created by all your past experiences – all the things you have felt, thought, seen, experienced and all the things others have told you or you have told yourself. You are what you have lived through but the question you need to ask yourself now is whether that person is a true reflection of who you are.

All of us get told things by other people when we grow up and the tendency when we are young and impressionable is to believe them. I know that a constant theme in my life has been trying to prove to myself first and then to others that I am not what they assumed or told me I was. When I was 16 years old and in love with books, I was told I should go into a class for less-able readers because I was not 'university material'. Five years later, after leaving school and home educating myself, I was awarded a place at King's College, Cambridge University reading Theology and English. I was told by the first agent and editor I approached with my book ideas that I wasn't going to make it as an author. I have now written over 100 books with sales of close to a million in total. I was told that there was no future for me in writing spiritual books. I hit the *Sunday Times* top 10 bestsellers twice. I could go on and on with things I have been told I couldn't do by someone and then found the resources within me to challenge that view.

If you have been repeatedly told during your childhood that you were not clever or that you were not good enough, these messages will have had an impact on the kind of adult you grew into. It is not just in childhood that we receive negative messages though – they happen at all ages and stages of our lives. Our minds can't tell the difference between fact and opinion and if you are constantly told, by others and yourself, that you are worthless, sooner or later your mind is made up. Don't let this get you despondent, though, or make you frightened of your thoughts and the voices of others. Quite the opposite. The suggestible nature of your mind is a reason to rejoice because it means that you can actually begin the process of positive change by changing the thoughts and words that you repeat to yourself.


## THE BENEFITS

'Affirmation without discipline is the beginning of delusion.'
Jim Rohn

The good news – the empowering news – is that you can change the way your mind is programmed in a very simple way and that is through the power of repeating positive statements to yourself. These are often called affirmations and science has confirmed their mighty power to transform lives. Evidence-based research has shown that affirmations, like prayer, can rewire the brain.[1] Affirmations interrupt and reorganize negative thought patterns that have established themselves over the years and replace them with new life-affirming beliefs. They help you take control and make your thoughts work for you rather than against you.

Earlier we saw that questions have even more power than affirmations (and that is why Ritual #3 was a life-changing question, see page 25) but we are at the end of the day now and your mind needs to relax and unwind and not be fired with the creativity to find answers. In other words, affirmations are not as powerful as questions but they are still mighty powerful and perfect for your evening rituals.

## ANECDOTAL EVIDENCE

'You will be a failure until you impress the subconscious with the conviction that you are a success. Making an affirmation that clicks does this.'

Florence Scovel Shinn

A year or so ago I had never given a talk in a bookshop or elsewhere about my books and my writing. The reason: I didn't believe I could do it or that anyone would want to come and hear me talk. I was content to work quietly and invisibly behind my computer. Then, as I described earlier in the book (see page 17), I was introduced to social media by one of my readers and soon discovered what a wonderful platform it was to communicate with my readers in such an immediate way. Having broken that barrier it was almost inevitable that I would soon be invited to give talks and workshops.

My first reaction was fear but I also sensed this was something I had to do. The world of publishing has changed and authors need to get out there but how did I overcome that fear? I read a lot of books about public speaking and asked authors I knew for advice. The best advice I got was to think positive thoughts and simply tell myself that I was an eloquent speaker and I was going to give a great talk.

It sounds simple but it absolutely worked and now, every time I give a talk, the night before I repeatedly tell myself out loud – so I get used to the sound of my voice without interruption – that I am a great public speaker and my audience will be informed and inspired by what I am going to tell them. I'm often asked back to places I have given author talks at, so although I may not inspire all who attend, this suggests to me that I'm doing something right.

# PRACTICE:
## SAY IT OUT LOUD

You've probably heard about the life-changing potential of affirmations before but have you actually tried them? Perhaps you feel faintly ridiculous talking to yourself out loud or don't quite believe something as simplistic as that can work so you've not experimented. But as this book is about doing rather than thinking about doing I am going to ask you for the next 21 days, as you are getting yourself undressed and ready for bed, to repeat to yourself out loud three times the following statement:

- 'I am the architect of my life; I build its foundation and choose its contents and my potential for happiness and success is limitless.'

- 'I am the architect of my life; I build its foundation and choose its contents and my potential for happiness and success is limitless.'

- 'I am the architect of my life; I build its foundation and choose its contents and my potential for happiness and success is limitless.'

## BRINGING THE RITUAL TO LIFE

'You can close the window and darken the room but you
can also open the window and let light in. It is a matter of
choice. Your mind is your room. Do you darken it or fill it
with light?'

Anonymous

Saying the above statement out loud ritualizes in your mind
for the following three reasons:

**First:** Saying something out loud starts to reprogramme
your mind to see what you are saying as absolute truth. The
words don't just come from your thoughts but from your
voice, giving them double the power. Once you start to truly
believe what you have said you are helping to manifest it to
reality.

**Second:** Using these affirmations before you go to bed rather
than first thing in the morning is more powerful because
what you say and think before you go to bed will be stored
in your unconscious and then when you fall asleep at night it
will inform your dreams. Just as a seed grows fastest during
the darkness the ideas in your mind take deep root while you
sleep. Then when you wake the next morning your mind is
one step closer to becoming convinced that you are telling it
the truth.

**Third:** I believe the above statement it is the most
empowering affirmation. Speak it and sleep on it every night
for three weeks and the message will become ingrained and
absorbed at an unconscious level so that you actually believe

it and when you believe something you start to take the action required to actually make it happen.

## DO IT: REPEAT AFTER ME!

Every instant of your life you can change your life by changing your focus, changing what that focus means to you and then, most important of all, changing what you are actually doing about it. I can think of no better way to sum up here than with this statement, which sounds like a Disney cliché but like many a cliché is profoundly true.

If you can dream it and believe in it you can do it.

'It is the repetition of affirmations that leads to belief. And once that belief becomes a deep conviction, things start to happen.'

Muhammad Ali

# LIFE-CHANGING RITUAL #**20**

# FLASH FORWARD

'To plant a garden is to believe in tomorrow.'

Audrey Hepburn

As the day draws to a close your thoughts will most likely turn at some point to the activities you have planned for tomorrow. This ritual asks you to visualize a successful day ahead and, if possible, to write down what you hope to achieve the next day as well. In this way, when you wake up your mind will be expecting you to have a brilliant day because you have told your unconscious mind that, come what may, tomorrow will be a satisfying and productive day.

The reason for doing this ritual just before you go to bed is that your mind is about to go to sleep – the time when your unconscious rules in dreams. This shutting-down phase between being wide awake and gently falling asleep, when you are still alert but also relaxing or unwinding, is the ideal time to plant suggestions in your mind so they are more likely to take hold. It is similar to the trance that hypnotherapists, such as Paul McKenna, induce in their clients.

## THE BENEFITS

'Tomorrow could be the someday you have been waiting for.'

Anonymous

Research shows that, alongside visualization, writing down your goals can increase your chances of achieving[1] them and so that's always advised. However, the important thing here is not so much the forward planning but to anticipate the outcome of whatever you have planned being overwhelmingly positive. As you visualize tell yourself that if something unexpected comes up you will deal with it successfully. You aren't a fortune-teller so, of course, you may find that what you visualize for the day ahead doesn't actually happen: for example, meetings get rearranged and travel plans may get frustrated, and so on, but the most important part of your visualization is that feeling of satisfaction and excitement about your day ahead. The feeling that whatever happens you will grow and learn from your day.

## ANECDOTAL EVIDENCE

'Life always gives you a second chance. It's called tomorrow.'

Anonymous

I described the power of visualization in Ritual #6 so you might also want to revisit the many benefits it can bring (see page 50) but I started doing flash-forward visualizations a few years ago and have been astonished by the results.

The great majority of my days now truly are happy and fulfilling ones, in contrast to previously when the outcome of each day very much felt like a lottery. I just close my eyes every night and tell myself how well everything is going to go tomorrow.

When I first heard about this technique I instantly realized that I had been going to bed most nights doing exactly the opposite: worrying about whether I would do well or achieve my goals; without realizing it I was visualising my tomorrow in a negative way. I got exactly what I had wished for the night before – my days weren't typically great ones and what happened to me felt very much like random chance or luck.

Of course, I accept that everything that happens in my day isn't going to be amazing just because I have visualized it the night before. I know that life is all about learning from our challenges and setbacks as well as our successes, but what this technique has taught me is just how important the way I think about or imagine the day ahead the night before is. If I choose the right attitude and perspective for my tomorrow the night before it truly changes how I interpret and create the following day. I don't feel a victim of circumstances or people or situations anymore. Come what may, I know I will find something positive and empowering in my day and it will be another stepping stone to success and happiness. What's more, it is simply blissful going to sleep knowing that when the alarm goes off I won't dread the start of a new day but be eager and excited to start it.

# PRACTICE: HOW TO VISUALIZE TOMORROW

The ideal time to do your forward planning for the day ahead is just before you go to bed or even sitting up in bed before you lie down to go to sleep. To ritualize your forward planning you need to visualize it happening. See yourself in your mind's eye experiencing the day and it being an amazing success. Don't just see it in your mind's eye – also hear it and feel it. Make it come alive as much as possible and fill it with deep meaning. If you have a meeting visualize the end of the meeting being a success with a firm shake of the hand and a smile. If you are giving a talk visualize it going brilliantly and everyone applauding at the end. If you have an exam visualize yourself being able to handle all the questions and having time to check your answers to your satisfaction. If you are going to a party visualize everyone enjoying your company and so on.

## BRINGING THE RITUAL TO LIFE

'Visualise this thing that you want. See it. Feel it. Believe in it. Make your mental blue print and begin to build.'

Robert Collier

If you have trouble visualizing a positive outcome, you might find it helpful to find some pictures online, which resemble the things you want to manifest in your life, to give your mind a visual trigger.

Remember, though, just looking at pictures isn't enough: you have to fully enter into the visualization with all your senses and thoughts. You have to make it come alive and feel real and one way to do that is to think of visualization as fun – a time for you to create a world where you are in control and feel great about everything you choose to bring into it. (See also Ritual #6, page 50.)

## DO IT: FLASH FORWARD!

Visualization isn't going to work without positive action but never, ever underestimate the power of your dreams and daydreams. So for the next 21 days, every night before you go to sleep, see your next day flowing perfectly. Feel all that you have planned unfolding the way you wish it to. See yourself gliding effortlessly and positively through a successful day.

If you can truly see it happening in your mind the night before, you have given your mind a glimpse of a potential future – a future that is both achievable and amazing and absolutely perfect for you.

'Whatever you can do, or dream you can do, begin it. Boldness has genius, power and magic in it. Begin it now.'

Goethe

# LIFE-CHANGING RITUAL #**21**

# SAY THANK YOU

'Gratitude opens to the door to... the power, the wisdom, the creativity of the universe. You open the door through gratitude.'

Deepak Chopra

This final ritual of your day is arguably the most powerful ritual of them all. It also couldn't be easier as it requires you to simply say thank you before you drift off to the land of sleep and dreams. You probably already intuitively sense that gratitude is a good thing to do but this ritual shows you that it is absolutely the right and perfect thing for you to do.

## THE BENEFITS

'It is not happiness that brings us gratitude. It's gratitude that brings us happiness.'

Anonymous

If you asked me what is the one single thing you can do that costs nothing and is easy to do that will make your life happier, healthier and more positive and successful, I would tell you that it would be to cultivate an attitude of gratitude.

Science has shown that being more grateful can make you healthier and happier and more positive.[1] It can help you achieve your goals because when you focus your thoughts and feelings on what you have to be thankful for, you are focusing your energy on what you want and therefore attracting more of it into your life. It improves your relationships because if you appreciate others they tend to reciprocate. It reduces negativity because it is very hard to be negative when you are feeling grateful, and, last but by no means least, it can also help you solve problems and learn new things because a grateful mind-set looks for new possibilities and sees opportunity in every challenge.

## ANECODOTAL EVIDENCE

'If the only prayer you said in your life was "Thank you" that would suffice.'

Master Eckhart

Only last week I had an amazing conversation with a barista while she was making my coffee. She asked me how I was and I said 'Fine' and asked her the same. She told me she was fine too but missed her family sometimes. I asked where her family was from and she told me they were from Poland. I asked her if she was making friends in the UK. She was silent for a few moments then said that she was gradually but couldn't understand why people in the UK weren't friendlier and happier people. She said she was from Poland and there were so many reasons to be friendly and happy to live here.

I was incredibly grateful for the reminder, as it is so easy to take things for granted.

# PRACTICE: HOW TO TAKE AN ATTITUDE OF GRATITUDE

The ideal time to perform this last ritual would be as you are lying in bed and just about to go to sleep, although if you are one of these people who fall asleep the moment their head touches the pillow then it might be better to do it when you are sitting up in bed before you lie down.

Just reflect for a few moments on what or whom you have to be grateful for in your life right now. Then allow yourself to bask in those good feelings for a few moments and say 'Thank you' either to yourself or, better still, out loud. However challenging or difficult your life currently is, there is always something that you can focus on for a few moments that you are grateful for. We often take for granted things that we should be grateful for like our health, the people or animals that love us or even the last meal we had. Just the fact that you are breathing is something to be grateful for because life is the most precious gift. Remember, to say you are grateful does not mean your life is perfect – it just means you are aware of your blessings.

## BRINGING THE RITUAL TO LIFE

'Feeling gratitude and not expressing it is like wrapping a present and not giving it.'

William Arthur Ward

### DO IT: SAY THANK YOU!

Find a few moments at the end of your day for the next 21 days to make gratitude for what you have rather than regret for what you don't have your entire focus. You will then melt into sleep with the 'miracles are possible' mind-set bringing magic and creativity to your dreams and will rise the next morning with an attitude of sincere appreciation.

So from now on, instead of waiting for something to happen to make you feel grateful, end your day with appreciation. In this way you will be on your way to becoming a master of gratitude with an abundant, happy and fulfilling life to match. You will be changing your life for the better one day and one thank you at a time.

'As we express our gratitude we must never forget that the highest appreciation is not to utter words but to live by them.'

John F. Kennedy

# EVENING CHECK POINT

Before you go to sleep review the seven rituals below to make sure you have completed them all.

For ease of reference you may want to photograph this list on your mobile or quickly jot them down on a piece of paper and place on your bedside table.

**Ritual #15: Over to you**

**Ritual #16: Say Grace**

**Ritual #17: Write it down**

**Ritual #18: Higher selfie**

**Ritual #19: Repeat after me**

**Ritual #20: Flash forward**

**Ritual #21: Say thank you**

And finally...

Don't forget to congratulate yourself on successfully completing your 21 daily rituals. Tomorrow is another day and it will be another day when you take positive action and start doing all that you can to make your dreams come true.

# AFTERWORD

# THE ADVENTURE BEGINS...

'The next message you need is always right where you are.'
Ram Dass

Writing this book has been unforgettable. I already knew the life-changing potential of ritual – and truly do live what I preach – but researching it and writing it down in a systemic way has reaffirmed that even more powerfully to me. I have all the proof I need that happiness and success is a choice and that the rituals in this book hold the key to a better and more meaningful life.

I sincerely hope you have incorporated the 21 rituals into your life for a minimum of 21 days. Congratulations if you have because the toughest part of your journey to happiness and success is over. It doesn't make sense to give up now because it is *now* that you will really begin to know yourself, love yourself and feel confident that you can live the life of your dreams.

At the end of your 21-day journey you will end at the beginning and not only know the place (yourself) for the first time but start to reap the benefits that the magical power of ritual performed over a period of three weeks can have on your life. Stay on your path to transformation and nothing in your life will ever feel the same again because from now on you will notice meaning and magic in every single thing. The ordinary will have become the extraordinary.

Exciting times lie ahead for you.

## THE WAY AHEAD

'Ritual is not simply an attitude or an intention, just as love is not a feeling. At its most basic, ritual is something that you do. A man can't plough a field just by thinking about it.'

Alison Lilly

It might help to join forces with other people who believe in the power of ritual to keep you company on your journey to transformation. You can share experiences and inspire each other and talk about your successes and triumphs. Keep the focus on what is positive not on what is negative and write a joyful future for yourselves. If it's not possible for you to connect with others in this way you'll find inspirational advice and motivation tips on my Theresa Cheung author page on Facebook or check out my website: www.theresacheung.com. Remember, too, you can always get in touch with me to discuss your progress and details about how to do that can be found on page 194.

Keep doing the 21 rituals until they become second nature and success and happiness is no longer a goal to be achieved but your natural state. Notice all the ways that your life starts to improve. And as you travel towards positive change never lose sight of the fact that you are what you repeatedly do.

Take action to bring what you want into your life rather than dreaming about it.

Never forget too that this isn't all about you. If you change your life for the better you remind others of their potential for greatness. Your inspiring example encourages them to become the best that they can be. It really can all start with *you* when you make that choice to not just think about but also actually become the change that you want to see in the world.

'The world can only be grasped by action, not by contemplation.'

Jacob Bronowski

# R E F E R E N C E S

## INTRODUCTION: 21 DAYS

1 Neal, D. *et al.* 'How do people adhere to goals when willpower is low?: The profits (and pitfalls) of strong habits', *American Journal of Personality and Social Psychology*, Jun 2013; 104(6): 959–75: doi: 10.1037/a0032626

2 Duhigg, C. *The Power of Habit: Why We Do What We Do in Life and Business* (Random House, 2012)

3 Coman, A. 'Designing personal grief rituals: An analysis of symbolic objects and actions', Lancaster University Research Portal, Death Studies, 19 June 2016: www.research.lancs.ac.uk/portal/en/publications/designing-personal-grief-rituals(6f440948-5f38-45aa-bad1-9573ecfad1c3).html

4 Lally, P. 'How are habits formed: Modelling habit formation in the real world', *European Journal of Social Psychology*, Oct 2010; 40(6): 998–1009

5 Gino, F. *Sidetracked: Why Our Decisions Get Derailed and How We Can Stick to the Plan* (Harvard Business Review Press, 2013)

6 Vohs, K. *et al.* 'Rituals enhance consumption', *Psychological Science*, Sep 2013; 24 (9): 1714–21: doi: 10.1177/0956797613478949

7 Bryant, F. *Savouring: A New Model of Positive Experience* (NJ Lawrence Eribaum Associates, 2007)

8 www.prevention.com/mind-body/emotional-health/double-your-happiness-through-savoring

9  Pennebaker, J. *Expressive Writing: Words that Heal* (Idyll, 2014)

10  www.scientificamerican.com/article/why-rituals -work/

11  www.bakadesuyo.com/2015/10/ritual/

12  Norton, M. and Gino, F. 'Rituals alleviate grieving for loved ones, loves and lotteries', *Journal of Experimental Psychology*, Feb 2014; 143(1): 266–72: doi: 10.1037/a0031772. Epub 11 Feb 2013

## LIFE-CHANGING RITUAL #1: WAKE UP EARLIER

1  https://hbr.org/2010/07/defend-your-research-the-early-bird-really-does-get-the-worm

2  www.webmd.com/food-recipes/most-important -meal#1

3  www.nytimes.com/1995/09/27/us/personal-health-debate-aside-melatonin-can-reset-the-body-s-clock.html

4  www.nytimes.com/2002/02/15/us/study-ties-6-7-hours-of-sleep-to-longer-life.html

## LIFE-CHANGING RITUAL #2: STRETCH INSTEAD OF REACHING FOR YOUR PHONE

1  www.dailymail.co.uk/health/article-2577824/Why-NEVER-mobile-bedroom.html

2  http://consumers.ofcom.org.uk/news/a-nation-addicted -to-smartphones/

3  www.telegraph.co.uk/technology/mobile-phones/11600815/Are-you-addicted-to-your-mobile-phone.html

4  https://sleepfoundation.org/ask-the-expert/electronics -the-bedroom

5  www.livestrong.com/article/430886-what-are-the-benefits-of-stretching-in-the-morning/

## LIFE-CHANGING RITUAL #3: ASK YOURSELF ONE SIMPLE QUESTION

1 Hagger, M. *et al.* 'Ego depletion and the strength model of self control: A meta-analysis University of Nottingham,' *Psychological Bulletin*, Jul 2010; 136(40): 495–525

2 Dispenza, J. *Evolve Your Brain: The Science of Changing Your Mind* (Health Communications, 2009)

3 Wood, E. *et al.* 'Positive self-statements: Power for some, peril for others', *Psychological Science*, Jul 2009, 20(7); 860–6

4 Senay, I. *et al.* 'Motivating goal-directed behavior through introspective self-talk: The role of the interrogative form of simple future tense', *Psychological Science*, Apr 2010; 21(4): 499–504

## LIFE-CHANGING RITUAL #4: JUST BREATHE

1 www.health.harvard.edu/mind-and-mood/relaxation-techniques-breath-control-helps-quell-errant-stress-response

2 www.amsa.org/healthy-exercises-to-start-the -year/

3 www.amsa.org/healthy-exercises-to-start-the -year/

## LIFE-CHANGING RITUAL #5: SMILE IN THE MIRROR

1 www.psychologicalscience.org/index.php/news/releases/smiling-facilitates-stress-recovery.html

2 www.aath.org/do-children-laugh-much-more-often -than-adults-do

3 www.smithsonianmag.com/science-nature/simply-smiling-can-actually-reduce-stress-10461286/?no-ist

4 http://healthland.time.com/2010/03/25/grinning-for-a -longer-life/

5  www.theatlantic.com/health/archive/2013/01/
   how-smiles-control-us-all/272588/
6  www.forbes.com/sites/rogerdooley/2013/02/26/
   fake-smile/#28d93c0334cd
7  https://www.researchgate.net/publication/51645748_
   Social_laughter_is_correlated_with_an_elevated_pain_
   threshold

## LIFE-CHANGING RITUAL #6: SEE THE FINISH LINE

1  Garfield, C. *Peak Performance: Mental Training Techniques
   of the World's Greatest Athletes* (Warner Books, 1984)
2  *Ibid.* 9
3  http://breakingmuscle.com/sports-psychology/the
   -history-science-and-how-to-of-visualization
4  Isaac, A. 'Mental Practice: Does it Work in the Field?',
   *Sport Psychologist*, 1992; 6(2): 192–8
5  http://umm.edu/Health/Medical/AltMed/Treatment/
   Mindbody-medicine
6  Verdelle, C. 'Effect of mental practice on the development
   of a certain motor skill', *Research Quarterly of the
   American Association for Health, PE and Recreation*, 1960;
   31(4): 560–9
7  Driskell, J. *et al.* 'Does mental practice enhance
   performance?' *Journal of Applied Psychology*, 1994; 79(4):
   481–92

## LIFE-CHANGING RITUAL #7: TUNE IN

1  Gerry, D. *et al.* 'Active Music classes in infancy enhance
   musical, communicative and social development',
   *Developmental Science*, May 2012; 15(3): 348–407
2  'Musical training can increase blood flow to the brain',
   British Psychological Society (BPS), 8 May 2014

3 Zuk, J. *et al.* 'Behavioural and neural correlates of executive functioning in musicians and non musicians', *PLoS ONE*, Jun 2014; 9(6): e99868.doi:10.1371/journal. pone 0099868

4 Jenkins, J. 'The Mozart effect', *Journal of the Royal Society of Medicine*, Apr 2001; 94(4): 170–2

5 Kanduri, C. *et al.* 'The effect of listening to music on human transcriptome', *PeerJ*, Mar 2015; 12(3): e830. doi: 10.7717/peerj.830

## LIFE-CHANGING RITUAL #8: TIDY ONE THING

1 https://www.sharecare.com/health/stress-reduction/article/the-health-benefits-of-decluttering

2 McMains, S. *et al.* 'Interactions of top down and bottom up mechanisms in human visual cortex', *J Neurosci,* Jan 2011; 31(2): 587–97

3 https://www.psychologytoday.com/blog/the-good-life/201207/home-clutter-confusion -and-chaos

4 www.aasmnet.org/articles.aspx?id=5619

5 Arnold, J. *Life at home in the Twenty First Century: 32 Families Open Their Doors* (EDS Publications Ltd, 2012)

## LIFE-CHANGING RITUAL #9: FILL YOUR OWN CUP

1 www.dailymail.co.uk/health/article-2828835/Tea-coffee-prefer-weight-loss-cancer-prevention-reveal-health-benefits-both.html

2 www.simplypsychology.org/self-esteem.html

## LIFE-CHANGING RITUAL #10: LET IT GO

1 https://www.researchgate.net/publication/26869816_Ironic_Effects_of_Emotion_Suppression_When_Recounting_Distressing_Memories

2  https://www.psychologytoday.com/blog/emotional
-freedom/201007/the-health-benefits-tears

## LIFE-CHANGING RITUAL #11: SAY A LITTLE PRAYER

1  Francis, L. *et al*. 'Prayer and psychological health: A
study among sixth form pupils attending Catholic and
Protestant schools in Northern Ireland', *Mental Health,
Religion and Culture*, 2008; 11(1): 85–92

2  www.health.harvard.edu/heart-health/
optimism-and-your-health

3  Wooe, W. *et al*. 'Habits in everyday life: Thought, emotion
and action', *J Pers Soc Psychol,* Dec 2002; 83(6): 1281–97

## LIFE-CHANGING RITUAL #12: LIGHT SOMEONE UP

1  www.psychologicalscience.org/index.php/news/
releases/the-power-of-suggestion-what-we-expect-
influences-our-behavior-for-better-or-worse.html

2  Michael, R. *et al*. 'Suggestion, Cognition, and Behavior',
*Current Directions in Psychological Science*, 2012; 21(3):
151–6

3  www.helpguide.org/articles/work-career/volunteering-
and-its-surprising-benefits.htm

4  https://www.psychologytoday.com/blog/high-octane-
women/201409/helpers-high-the-benefits-and-risks
-altruism

5  www.ncbi.nlm.nih.gov/pubmed/22642341

6  http://greatergood.berkeley.edu/article/item/the_
activism_cure/

7  https://helix.northwestern.edu/article/kindness-
contagious-new-study-finds

### LIFE-CHANGING RITUAL #13: LISTEN, REALLY LISTEN

1  http://hbr.org/2014/01/three-ways-leaders-can-listen
   -with-more-empathy

### LIFE-CHANGING RITUAL #14: RIGHT HERE, RIGHT NOW

1  http://mrsmindfulness.com/ted-talk-happiness-is
   -mindfulness/
2  www.helpguide.org/harvard/benefitsofmindfulness.htm
3  http://berkeleysciencereview.com/can-mindfulness-
   make -you-happier/

### LIFE-CHANGING RITUAL #15: OVER TO YOU

1  http://hbr.org/2012/01/the-surprising-benefits-of-sol.
   html

### LIFE-CHANGING RITUAL #16: SAY GRACE

1  https://www.human.cornell.edu/pam/outreach/upload/
   Family-Mealtimes-2.pdf

### LIFE-CHANGING RITUAL #17: WRITE IT DOWN

1  www.forbes.com/sites/elevate/2014/04/08/why-you-
   should-be-writing-down-your-goals/#58c6b0c2f141
2  http://Blogs.scientificamerican.com/beautiful-minds/
   the-real-neuroscience-of-creatiityy/

### LIFE-CHANGING RITUAL #18: HIGHER SELFIE

1  Baumeister, R. *et al*. 'Does high self-esteem cause
   better performance, interpersonal success or healthier
   lifestyles?' *Psychological Science in the Public Interest*, May
   2003; 4(91): 1–44

2  https://www.psychologytoday.com/blog/the-attraction-doctor/201105/is-your-personality-making-you-more-or-less-physically-attractive

3  Kniffin, K. and Wilson, D. 'The effect of nonphysical traits on the perception of physical attractiveness: Three naturalistic studies', *Evolution and Human Behavior*, 2004; 25: 88–101

4  Swami, V. *et al*. 'More than just skin deep?: Personality information influences men's ratings of the attractiveness of women's body sizes', *Journal of Social Psychology*, 2010; 150(6): 6280674

5  Lewandowski, G. *et al*. 'Personality goes a long way: The malleability of opposite-sex physical attractiveness', *Personal Relationships*, 2007; 14: 571–85

## LIFE-CHANGING RITUAL #19: REPEAT AFTER ME

1  https://www.psychologytoday.com/blog/wired-success/201305/do-self-affirmations-work-revisit

## LIFE-CHANGING RITUAL #20: FLASH FORWARD

1  www.researchgate.net/publication/247895325_The_Health_Benefits_of_Writing_about_Life_Goals

## LIFE-CHANGING RITUAL #21: SAY THANK YOU

1  www.health.harvard.edu/newsletter_article/in-praise-of-gratitude

# SELECT BIBLIOGRAPHY

Arnold, J. *Life at Home in the Twenty First Century: 32 Families Open Their Doors* (EDS Publications Ltd, 2012)

Byrant, F. *Savouring: A New Model of Positive Experience* (Psychology Press, 2006)

Byrne, R. *The Secret* (Beyond Words Publishing, 2006)

Dispenza, J. *Evolve Your Brain: The Science of Changing Your Mind* (Health Communications, 2009)

Duhigg, C. *The Power of Habit: Why We Do What We Do in Life and Business* (Random House, 2012)

Garfield, C. *Peak Performance: Mental Training Techniques of the World's Greatest Athletes* (Warner Books, 1984)

Gino, F. *Sidetracked: Why our Decisions Get Derailed and How We Can Stick to Our Plan* (Harvard Business Review, 2013)

Hay, L. *You Can Heal Your Life* (Hay House, 1984)

Kingston, K. *Clear Your Clutter with Feng Shui* (Three Rivers Press, 1999)

Korb, A. *The Upward Spiral: Using Neuroscience to Reverse the Course of Depression One Small Change at a Time* (New Harbinger, 2015)

Maltz M. *Psycho-Cybernetics: A New Way to Get More Living Out of Life* (Pocket Books, 1989)

Morris, T. *Feng Shui Your Life: The Quick Guide to Decluttering Your Home and Renewing Your Life* (Turner, 2011)

Mckenna, P. *I Can Make You Happy* (Bantam Press, 2011)

Newberg, A. *How Enlightenment Changes Your Brain: The New Science of Transformation* (Avery, 2016)

Pennebaker, J. *Expressive Writing: Words that Heal* (Idyll, 2014)

Ratey, J. *Spark: The Revolutionary New Science of Exercise and the Brain* (Little, Brown, 2008)

Robbins, A. *Unleash the Power Within* (Nightingale Conant, 1999)

Rock, D. *Your Brain at Work: Strategies for Overcoming Distraction, Regaining Focus and Working Smarter All Day Long* (Harper, 2009)

Wiseman, R. *The Luck Factor* (Arrow Books, 2004)

# ABOUT THE AUTHOR

Feel free to get in contact with me if you have any questions, insights or experiences to share but, to risk repeating myself, please don't get in touch unless you have completed the rituals in this book for a minimum of 21 days.

The best place to reach me is to comment or message me on my Theresa Cheung author page on Facebook or via the contact form on my website www.theresacheung.com. Alternatively, write to me, care of Watkins Media Limited, Angel Business Club, 359 Goswell Road, London EC1V 7JL.

I truly welcome all your feedback but whether you decide to get in touch with me or not I hope this book has opened your mind to the idea that actions speak so much louder than words or thoughts and if those actions are ritualized and filled with personal meaning they have the power to change your life for the better.

'You never change your life until you change something you do daily. The secret of your success is found in your daily routine.'

John C. Maxwell

'Ritual is the passageway of the soul into the infinite.'

Algernon Blackwood